IN FELONY'S MIRROR
Reflections on Pain and Promise

A memoir with essays on
legal ethics and restorative justice,
for policy makers and classrooms

For Charlie,
with Eternal
gratitude - still
intent on paying you
back in spades!
Michael

IN FELONY'S MIRROR
Reflections on Pain and Promise

A memoir with essays on
legal ethics and restorative justice,
for policy makers and classrooms.

Michael Sweig, JD
Metropolitan State College of Denver

IN FELONY'S MIRROR: REFLECTIONS ON PAIN AND PROMISE

First Edition

Michael Sweig

I am First Amendment. Justice Greg Hobbs. Colorado Supreme Court. Reprinted with Permission.

Cover Photo Credit: Caron Legal | Sunset Beach, Ca.
Author Photo Credit: Carol Wynne Bailey

ISBN: 978-1466206991
ISBN-10: 1466206993
BISAC: Law / Essays
        Social Science / Criminology

Praise for "IN FELONY'S MIRROR"

"...[A] powerful piece of writing.... It offers no easy explanations for the moral complexities of life."

> Donald H. Whitfield
> Director of Adult Education Programs
> The Great Books Foundation

"Excellent for policy makers, Bar leaders, and teachers or students of ethics, criminal justice, business and law."

> Mark Whitacre, ADM whistleblower
> profiled in the movie, "The Informant"

"Sweig is dedicated to solutions that allow everyone to win."

> Sue Paige, Co-Founder-Owner
> Pathways to Successful Living

"Non-stop thrilling, insightful and refreshing. Sweig's level of self-disclosure exposes the compromising world of wealth. His description of entropy is so useful because he doesn't shift blame. And he challenges Republican and Democratic attacks on the rights of ex-offenders."

> Gregory T. Williams
> Milwaukee Area Workforce Investment Board

ALSO BY THE AUTHOR

RECENT PUBLIC POLICY PUBLICATIONS

"MOVING THE BOX" BY EXECUTIVE ORDER IN ILLINOIS | De Paul Journal for Social Justice, 4 DePaul J. for Soc. Just. 1:17 Fall 2010. (with co-author, Melissa McClure)

BLUEPRINT FOR PROGRESS: HOW ILLINOIS EMPOWERS REHABILITATED PEOPLE WITH CRIMINAL RECORDS | Ch. 8, ISSUES WITH CRIMINAL RECORDS, 2010 Supplement, Illinois Institute of Continuing Legal Education | SUMMER 2010

BEYOND LEGAL MECHANISMS – EMPLOYMENT, HOUSING AND OTHER SUPPORTS | Ch. 6, ISSUES WITH CRIMINAL RECORDS, 2010 Supplement, Illinois Institute of Continuing Legal Education | SUMMER 2010 (with co-author, Jodina Hicks)

OTHER WORKS

LIFE IN REVIEWS (2007 - 2011)

MAZIK

FOR MY OLDEST FRIENDS

Peter | Philip | Van | Charlie

IN LOVING MEMORY

Eli Blumberg
Mike Coffield
Jeff Paige

NOTE

I've changed nothing germane to protect anyone.

I blame no one for anything.

CONTENTS

FOREWARD

By Paul Karsten Fauteck, PsyD, DASB*

Michael Sweig doesn't carry scars from gunshot wounds or knife fights, nor has he had his cranium creased by a lead pipe. Yet if you study him carefully enough, you can see a layer of sadness somewhere below his polite-but-casual demeanor, and glimpse a tough resilience combined with a mix of acceptance and determination. So it's no surprise to learn he has survived different kinds of deep wounds: having and then losing wealth, position, respect, reputation, and a promising legal career.

Here Michael tells of his rise and fall and redemption step-by-step. He details the culture of "voodoo ethics," in which the bothersome issues of right and wrong disappear in a fog of legal technicalities and financial mazes. And, he describes that slippery slope of temporary solutions to long-term problems, when one gets too busy outrunning the inevitable to stop and think: "Wait! This is a crime!"

---

* Licensed clinical and forensic psychologist (ret.), former Senior Psychologist for the Department of Forensic Clinical Services, Circuit Court of Cook County (IL), and author of Going Straight: An Ex-Convict/Psychologist Tells Why and How. San Jose, Ca: Writers Club Press, 2001.

In the saga of Michael's professional life, there were numerous "villains" in a milieu that sets the stage for white-collar crime as surely as a gang-dominated neighborhood sets the stage for violence. He doesn't excuse himself or shift blame. And, perhaps most painful for him, he knows the one villain who could have stopped it all but didn't, is the man he sees in the mirror. But he minces no words in telling us this could happen to virtually any attorney, and perhaps does happen much more than we imagine.

Michael has kept some of his greatest possessions: intelligence, eloquence, vast legal knowledge, and enviable capacity for hard work. Rather than pursue the most lucrative possible application of these, he has concerned himself most with criminal justice reform and lowering of barriers society puts in the paths of convicted felons seeking pro-social lives. He makes an impassioned plea that we stop imprisoning more of our citizens than any other nation, and presents a compelling case for handling white-collar criminals as a valuable resource.

The knowledge and skill required to become a lawyer or physician doesn't evaporate instantly when one is convicted of a felony. It is morally wrong and financially irresponsible to let their preparation go to waste.

I predict the reader will find this work enjoyable and highly informative thanks to Michael's extensive research and numerous citations. Some graduate students may find he's done 25% of their dissertation for them.

The reader should also find what Michael tells us somewhat unsettling. Improvements in society come from courage, not complacency.

Paul Karsten Fauteck
Chicago, Illinois
November 2011

*   *

FOREWARD

by Rabbi Michael R. Zedek*

When Michael Sweig approached me with a request to write a brief reflection about a concept in Judaism called "Tikkun Olam," I was pleased to comply. However, our conversation about his work caused my notion of what I might say to acquire an added dimension and, perhaps, urgency.

Judaism focuses considerable attention on what it judges as the difference between the world as it is and the world as it should be. Further, Judaism insists we have a responsibility to bridge some of that distance. "Tikkun Olam" is shorthand for that commitment. It means "repairing the world," as in the world is fractured; broken in too many places. We have a responsibility; a duty to get to work to help restore some of those broken places and persons.

---

* Senior Rabbi, Emanuel Congregation. Chicago, Illinois.

As to Michael's work, the notion of repairing the world suggests criminal justice isn't just or primarily about punishment, even when it may or should include punishment. Rather, justice in the criminal law in the deepest sense also calls for us to restore fragments to wholeness. To the extent we are able, our task is making things and persons whole again.

So, to evaluate our criminal justice system by what it produces rather than by what it claims to do, the conclusion is inescapable: the current setting has very little to do with justice (the world as it should be); unless we embrace a dystopian vision of a world in which at any particular time a significant portion of the population is either incarcerated or entwined in an endlessly revolving door exiting and re-entering prison. And, while this structure seems well-suited for warehousing human beings and for some notions of retribution, we are all victims of our current approach; from those in prison who have earned such isolation, to those of us who worry fearfully, whether on the street or at home, about being safe from the predators who may be among us.

Michael's experience in this dysfunctional system and his wisdom derived from and despite the encounter suggests options that with our determination will save significant dollars (regrettably, a likely motivation for embracing any alternative, let alone promoting the political climate in which to discuss change).

More dramatically, Michael's suggestions provide a path for more of us to participate in the world as it could and should be; a world that includes persons and places that will be a bit more whole, and even perhaps, holy.

Rabbi Michael R. Zedek
Chicago, Illinios
November 2011

*   *

THE DIFFERENCE BETWEEN HEAVEN AND HELL

The residents of both Heaven and Hell sit at identical banquet tables with endless fresh breads, meats, fish, fruits, vegetables, nectars, wine, juice, water, and sweets, too.

In both Heaven and Hell, everyone has their arms in splints. No one can bend their arms to eat or drink.

In Hell, everyone is starving and eternally wretched.

In Heaven, everyone is well nourished, happy, and eternally peaceful.

In Hell, no one feeds their neighbors.

In Heaven, everyone feeds each other.

Adapted from a story Rabbi Lawrence Kushner told us in Torah School, at Congregation Solel, in the early 1970's.

INTRODUCTION

> He who opens a school door, closes a prison.
>
> Victor Hugo

Many readers know the Ad Council's legendary campaign slogan for the United Negro College Fund: "A Mind is a Terrible Thing to Waste." This gem of American vernacular applies to all minds, including white-collar minds.

But I'm not talking about a Madoff or Kozlowski as I tell my disbarred felon story to argue that some white-collars are crucial renewable resources whose education and skills should be deployed to educate less educated "other-collars," to act as agents of improvement on behalf of the justice system, and when possible to restore the direct victims and communities we have harmed. I am talking about people like me.

Readers who tolerate ambiguity may see my offenses as brazen, but may feel I offended in grey areas of business, law and life. Black-and-white readers may be appalled by my argument: as part of our criminal sentences and beyond, felons like me should be *empowered* to improve and heal the world in important ways. Some readers will agree; some won't know what to think.

Our criminal justice system is broken because it continues to break people and harm communities through the systematic disenfranchisement of millions of minds. But we are not bound to this path.

There are social justice and restorative solutions that are neither inherently conservative nor liberal, but are uniquely bi-partisan, because they address leveling the education and employment opportunity playing fields for millions more Americans who could then pay taxes and support their families. Our broken criminal justice system is one of our few gigantic messes we can actually fix by helping vulnerable populations without creating entitlements or other fiscal burdens. That is true social justice.

In the context of criminal justice reform, and especially in election cycles, social and restorative justice should rightly be both a conservative and liberal cause unrelated to redistribution of wealth. It has everything to do with honest second chances that enhance our economy, advance the common good and keep government smaller and costing everyone less.

Do we want educated, capable white-collars and other-collars costing taxpayers money while socially unproductive in prison cells or unemployed; or, do we want us civically engaged and working to help heal the communities we harmed, especially when restorative justice practices reduce recidivism?[1]

America has 5 percent of the world's population, 25 percent of prisoners worldwide, nearly 2.4 million incarcerated, and the world's highest incarceration rate, which has tripled in 20 years.[2] Between 2003 and 2011, the number of Americans with some kind of criminal record increased by the equivalent of 90% of America's entire population growth during that same period. America grew by 22 million people in those years, during which we added 20 million people to the rolls of people with criminal records.

In 2003, 24.45% of the US population had a criminal record. Currently, 29% of the US

---

[1] As I discuss in Part II.C, "Restorative Justice for White-Collar Crime," *infra* at 151, I am not a "restorative justice fundamentalist" as others

[2] The Pew Center on the States, One in 100: Behind Bars in America 2008, 3-4 (2008). http://www.pewcenteronthestates.org/uploadedFiles/8 015PCTS_Prison08_FINAL_2-1-1_FORWEB.pdf.

population has a criminal record:[3] about 92 million Americans—more than one in four adults.[4] This figure hovered around 71 million eight years ago, in 2003.[5]

About 700,000 people are released from state and federal prisons annually, and approximately 12 million are released from local jails, meaning at the state level alone, we arrest about 3%-5% of the American population, annually.[6]

---

[3] *See* US Population figures, Indexmundi.comhttp://www.indexmundi.com/g/g.aspx?v=21&c=us&l=en

[4] *See* "From Jail to Jobless: EEOC considers revising guidelines for criminal background checks. Nat'l Law Journal, August 9, 2011.

[5] United States Department of Justice, Office of Justice Programs, Attorney General Ashcroft Announces Nationwide Effort To Reintegrate Offenders Back Into Communities, www.reentry.gov/ashcroftpr.html.

[6] *See, e.g.* Seanna Adcox, Sentencing Reform Passes, The Associated Press, (Mar. 26, 2010), http://www.thesunnews.com/2010/03/26/1388199/sentencing-reform-passes.html; Shira Schoenberg, Prison Reform A Slow Train, Concord Monitor (Apr 23, 2010),http://www.concordmonitor.com/apps/pbcs.dll/article?AID=/20100423/FRONTPAGE/4230308; Randal C. Archibold, California in Financial Crisis, Opens Prisons, The New York Times, (Mar. 23, 2010),http://www.nytimes.com/2010/03/24/us/24calprisons.html. U.S. Department of Justice, Office of Justice Programs, Reentry, http://www.reentry.gov/ (visited on April 29, 2010); Allen J. Beck, The

As of 2006, America had a "felon class" of more than 16 million felons, representing 7.5 percent of the adult population..."[7] This number is likely closer to 20 million felons today.

Despite our record setting incarceration levels, probation is our most common criminal sentence; we have approximately 7 million Americans under correctional supervision,[8] roughly 5 million of whom are on probation at any given time.[9] Probationers in America increased 264% from

---

Importance of Successful Reentry to Jail Population Growth, Jail Reentry Roundtable of the Urban Institute, Washington, DC (June 27, 2006).

[7] Christopher Uggen, Jeff Manza & Melissa Thompson, Citizenship, Democracy, and the Civic Reintegration of Criminal Offenders, 605 ANNALS AM. ACAD. POL. & SOC. SCI. 281 (2006). In 2008, about one in 33 working-age adults was an ex-prisoner; one in 15 was a felon. Among working-age men that year, about one in 17 was an ex-prisoner and one in eight was a felon. *Id*.

[8] *Id*.

[9] Petteruti, A. (2011). Finding Direction: Expanding Criminal Justice Options by Considering Policies of Other Nations. Justice Policy Institute. Washington, DC.http://justicepolicy.org/uploads/justicepolicy/docu ments/finding_direction-full_report.pdf. *See also*, Glaze, Lauren E. Thomas P. Bonczar, and Fan Zhang. 2010.Probation and Parole in the United States, 2009. Washington, DC: Bureau of Justice Statistics. NCJ 231674 Bulletin.

1980 to 2003.[10] By 1997 there were more than 2000 probation agencies and 50,000 probation officers.[11]

Unemployment among Americans with criminal records exceeds 50%.[12]   Prison records and felony convictions so greatly impair lawbreakers' employment prospects that America sustains between $57 billion and $65 billion annually in lost output.[13]

---

[10] Bureau of Justice Statistics. 2004. Probation and Parole in the United States, 2003. Washington, D.C.

[11] Patersilia, Joan. 1997. Probation in the United States. Pp. 149-200 in Crime and Justice: A Review of Research, vol. 22, edited by Michael Tonry. Chicago: University of Chicago Press.

[12] *Id.*

[13] *Id.*, at n. 11.

Americans with criminal records (who do have a legal right to work here) exceed undocumented workers,[14] and those Americans lacking any or enough health insurance.[15]

Conventional criminal justice practice, public policy, and social and corporate attitudes toward felons marginalize us so we can't work,[16] pay our own bills, care for our families, pay taxes, or

---

[14] A Bear Stearns report in 2005 estimated approximately 20 million. http://www.illegalaliens.us/images/Bear%20Stearns%20Study.pdf

[15] Approximately 29 million under-insured. 52 million uninsured. C. Schoen, M. M. Doty, R.H. Robertson, and S.R. Collins, "Affordable Care Act Reforms Could Reduce the Number of Underinsured U.S. Adults by 70 Percent," Health Affairs, Sept. 2011 30(9): 1762–71.

[16] States Help Ex-Inmates Find Jobs http://www.nytimes.com/2011/01/25/business/25offender.html?_r=3&pagewanted=all

maintain modern luxuries like higher education[17] or health insurance.[18]

We just can't afford traditional punishments, like overly long incarcerations and staining one-time, non-violent or low level lawbreakers with lifelong felony brands and stigmas.

In the best economic times, but worse in precarious times like these, this is too much potential brainpower to waste. If we're not careful, it's certainly too much mischief walking the streets with too little to do.

With essentially complete disregard for the common good, we have marginalized nearly one third of America and likely 20 million felons whom current law, sentencing practices, and rampant legal discrimination in education, employment and housing prevent from

---

[17] Higher education is already a luxury for people who do not have added obstacles like a criminal record. *See, e.g.*, Zoe Mendelson, "Admitted But Broke," OpEd, Los Angeles Times, August 24, 2008. http://articles.latimes.com/2008/aug/24/news/OE-MENDELSON24

[18] John Schmitt and Kris Warner. "Ex-Offenders and the Labor Market." The Center for Economic Policy and Research. Nov. 2010, http://www.cepr.net/documents/publications/ex-offenders-2010-11.pdf

becoming part of any solution to this problem, or to any other problems.[19]

Without extraordinary effort and against horrid odds, we are essentially disenfranchised from using our minds for the better. That's why I wrote this book.

If we want not to waste good minds and thereby to avoid the same old problems of crime, punishment, more crime and embittered victims, at least one solution is rooted in the concept of

---

[19] Post-conviction discrimination of felons is widely addressed in vast academic literature. I've also discussed it elsewhere. *E.g.*, Sweig, Michael. BEYOND LEGAL MECHANISMS – EMPLOYMENT, HOUSING AND OTHER SUPPORTS | Ch. 6, ISSUES WITH CRIMINAL RECORDS, 2010 Supplement, Illinois Institute of Continuing Legal Education | SUMMER 2010 (with co-author, Jodina Hicks).

"communitarianism,"   i.e.,   advancing   the common good.[20]

My focus is thus how we use the minds of appropriate lawbreakers to help seize restoration from harm, and develop better practices for responding to serious ethical transgressions in the legal profession and in white-collar sentencing, particularly in probation sentences.

Our goal must be for capable, skilled, educated lawbreakers like me to make not just victims "whole" if ever possible, but also to make the *community* more "whole."[21]

---

[20] Amitai Etzioni, A 308. "Communitarianism," Encyclopedia of Community: From the Village to the Virtual World, Vol 1, A-D, Karen Christensen and David Levinson, eds. (Sage Publications, 2003) pp. 224-228. "Communitarianism is a social philosophy that maintains that society should articulate what is good—that such articulations are both needed and legitimate. Communitarianism is often contrasted with classical liberalism, a philosophical position that holds each individual should formulate the good on his or her own. Communitarians examine the ways shared conceptions of the good (values) are formed, transmitted, justified, and enforced. Hence their interest in communities (and moral dialogues within them), historically transmitted values and mores, and the societal units that transmit and enforce values such as the family, schools, and voluntary associations (social clubs, churches, and so forth), which are all parts of communities."

[21] Restorative justice has existed for centuries with roots in tribal dispute resolution, practiced worldwide,

The key variables in this restorative equation are how best, on a case-by-case basis, (i) to *empower the lawbreaker* as part of his or her consequence to achieve victim restitution, i.e., "reparation," (ii) to achieve a degree of reconciliation if possible – depending on the victim's attitude or willingness, and (iii) to deploy the lawbreaker as human capital who works on behalf of the justice system to find or develop at least incremental

---

and can be called a resurging early-21st Century social movement. "Signs of restorative justice have...been detected in the practices of 'ancient Arab, Greek, and Roman civilizations,' of the 'Germanic peoples who s wept across Europe',.. 'Indian Hindus as ancient as the Vedic civilization...and ancient Buddhist, Taoist, and Confucian traditions.' Likewise, restorative justice has been discovered in the practices of the 'Aboriginals, the Inuit, and the native Indians of North and South America.'" Stephen P. Garvey, The Practice of Restorative Justice: Restorative Justice, Punishment, and Atonement, 2003 UTAH LAW REVIEW 303, 304. *See also*, Umbreit, M. S., Vos, B., & Coates, R. (2005). Restorative justice in the 21st century: A social movement full of opportunities and pitfalls. Marquette University Law Review, 89(2), 251-304. What's newer is the notion that application of restorative justice principles has potential value to white-collar crime. *See* Zvi D. Gabbay, "Holding Restorative Justice Accountable," 8 Cardozo J. Conflict Resol. 85 (2007); "Exploring the Limits of the Restorative Justice Paradigm: Restorative Justice and White-Collar Crime," 8 Cardozo J. Conflict Resol. 421 (2007); and Justifying Restorative Justice: A Theoretical Justification for the Use of Restorative Justice Practices, 2005 J. DISP. RESOL. 349, 350.

solutions to the systemic problems that allowed the lawbreaker's crime.[22]

This would be restoration to advance the common good. Plain old punishment is just punishment and accomplishes little if anything but depletion of the common good.[23]

---

[22] Hundreds of federal economic offenses constitute over 25% of all federal offenses. Economic crimes cover a broad range of conduct; the pertinent legal provisions protect many important interests that transcend victims' direct interests, like the integrity of financial and commodity markets, the judicial and political systems, etc.. The harm caused by economic offenses "often extends far beyond monetary losses to loss of jobs, homes, solvency, access to health care or financial security in retirement." Frank O. Bowman, The 2001 Federal Economic Crime Sentencing Reforms: An Analysis and Legislative History, 35 IND. L. REV. 5, 17 (2001).

[23] See Zvi D. Gabbay, Justifying Restorative Justice: A Theoretical Justification for the Use of Restorative Justice Practices, Id., at n.21. (empirical evidence demonstrates that restorative justice better reduces recidivism and promotes justice and fairness than traditional retributive criminal "justice").

We can't repair injured people and communities if all we do is punish lawbreakers.[24],[25] This is neither a soft-on-crime concept nor an argument that white-collars should not be punished.

---

[24] As distinct from punishment, rehabilitation and restoration are different but related. It's useful to think of them together, because while restoration addresses the community as part of one's criminal sentence, we must still consider the impact on the community if a lawbreaker can't find post-sentence employment. *See generally*, Pogarsky, G. (2006). Criminal records, employment, and recidivism. Criminology & Public Policy. 5:3. Andrew von Hirsch & Martin Wasik, Civil Disqualification Attending Conviction: A Suggested Conceptual Framework, 56 Cambridge L.J. 599, 605 (1997). cited in Margaret Colgate Love, "Starting Over With a Clean Slate: In Praise of a Forgotten Section of the Model Penal Code," 30 Fordham Urban Law Journal 101 (2003). Corrections Today, April 1, 87-92.; Krienert, J. & Fleisher, M. (2001). Economic rehabilitation: A reassessment of the link between employment and crime. Corrections Management Quarterly, 5 (4), 5.

[25] Gabbay, Justifying Restorative Justice, *Id.*, n. 21 at 375–390 (restorative justice consistent with retributive and utilitarian principles). The two philosophical premises of retributive theory (punishment according to just desserts and that fits the crime) might seem facially problematic for applying restorative justice to white-collar crime, but not really. It makes practical sense to determine what a "deserved" punishment actually is for each offense. *See* IMMANUEL KANT, THE METAPHYSICAL ELEMENTS OF JUSTICE 100–102 (1797), trans. John Ladd, (Macmillan Publishing Comp. 1986).

Doing the right thing from a policy standpoint should no longer mean simply punish the wrongdoer. Moreover, when dealing with lawyers like me, who break the law like I did, a close look at ethical sabotage and evaporation is warranted to see where it came from, and maybe find some solutions.

"Voodoo Ethics" discusses ethical vagaries. (Part II.B) It's not just the criminal justice system that should assess possible restorative solutions when a lawyer turns lawbreaker. The legal profession as an institution should do the same, rather than follow the traditional "punishment only" example set by the criminal justice system. "Legal" ethics are too often voodoo ethics as practiced by far too many law practitioners, because when applied "legal" ethics too often result in harm, not good. I know. I was the king of voodoo ethics, and from reflecting on this experience I offer restorative solutions.

"Restorative Justice for White-Collar Crime" (Part II.C) explores how restorative justice and civic engagement elements in white-collar crime sentencing can combine with traditional punishments to advance the common good (heal victims, communities, and employ former lawbreakers). The most common forms of civic engagement – associating, serving, giving and leading – offer realistic and inexpensive avenues to utilize, rather than waste, the many good minds of Americans with criminal records.

*   *

So, what can people with criminal records repair in exile? Not much.

The question of what would have been a just solution both to repair the direct harm I caused, rightly punish me yet also empower me still to contribute to the common good is, I feel, the best and least asked question. I'm advancing the common good now, in my life and with works like this one. But it's been a perilous path, way too long in coming, and has been to the advantage of far too few. I don't want this for my brothers and sisters with felony convictions or ruinous legal ethics transgressions. It's unnecessary and unwise.

I engage this conversation with personal narrative and scholarship. I explain events in my law firm that can and do happen in many law firms and businesses. My hope is with discussion among policy-makers and in classrooms, I can help make things much more right.

As my reflections and story unfold, the reader may feel I vacillate between claiming individual responsibility for my actions while repeatedly

emphasizing   powerful   influences   that
determined both my choices and the unraveling
of order. For me it's not vacillating. I reconcile
the two. I'm totally to blame in how I made a
mess of my life and harmed others. I didn't use
my energy to infuse enough order to put the
brakes on an increasingly slippery slope toward
chaos.

My own sense of what I was to achieve in my
mid to late thirties reflects an identity drowning
in unholy emulation of vapid upper middle class
values: pursuit of money as a basis for self-worth
and measure.

So, I was too weak to seize key moments when I
approached the crossroads of integrity or hell. I
chose hell because I didn't know I could fail in
my business without failing personally. Instead I
failed personally trying to advance a business
that had no ultimate spiritual or personal
meaning, except in the lessons of its failure.

But, with the help of so many people, in sharing
the lessons of my own failures I offer what I
hope is a contribution to help other people with
criminal records, especially those who are far less
privileged.

As an academic work, at best this is a primer; hardly comprehensive or definitive, yet a jumpstart to sensitize students and policy makers.

Maybe with conversations like this one there will be fewer people who put or find themselves in such legally and morally untenable binds. Maybe with thought about how we approach crime and the common good, there will be fewer minds to waste.

Michael Sweig
Denver, Colorado
November 5, 2011

*   *

REFLECTIONS

"We tell ourselves stories in order to live."

- Joan Didion, The White Album (1979)

"Their story, yours, mine - it's what we carry
with us on this trip we take, and we owe it to
each other to respect our stories and learn
from them."

- William Carlos Williams in
  Robert Coles, The Call of Stories: Teaching
  and the Moral Imagination (1989)

When I told a Senator who befriended me as a
new lobbyist the story of my disbarment and
related felony, he thanked me for my candor and
observed: "Most everyone has a background.
Not everyone's background is memorialized."

We are all better than our worst acts. The best
of us can do incredibly bad things. Just a
smidgeon of wrong influence, voodoo ethics and
the convergence of circumstance can lead to epic
personal transgressions and far-reaching disaster.

Like many white-collars, I was born privileged.[26] Yet I'm a boy-next-door type; not from the cabal of "crooked corporate tycoons, document-shredding Big Five accountants, and devious fat cats with offshore accounts."[27]

As with so many white-collars, for certain periods of my life I abused this privilege with horrid hubris.[28] For many people, I am and will remain controversial. I've caused a lot of trouble and to some harm, which regrettably I cannot reverse.

---

[26] "White-collar" entered the lexicon on December 27, 1939, when sociology professor Edwin Sutherland first used and defined the phrase when he addressed the American Sociological Society in Philadelphia: "a crime committed by a person of respectability and high social status in the course of his occupation." Sutherland, Edwin H. (1949). White Collar Crime. New York: Holt, Rinehart and Winston. Professor Sutherland's classist definition must be taken in the context of his era. He limits white-collars to a particular social stature, which is unworkable jurisprudence, since his definition seems to determine the lawbreaker's criminal liabiliy based on social status and not the offending conduct. *See* Baker, John. "The Sociological Origins of White Collar Crime," Legal Memorandum No. 14, The Heritage Foundation, Oct. 14,2004.
http://www.heritage.org/research/reports/2004/10/the-sociological-origins-of-white-collar-crime

[27] Frank O. Bowman, Are We Really Getting Tough on White Collar Crime? Hearing Before the Subcomm. on Crime and Drugs, S. Judiciary Comm. Part 2, 15 FED.SENT.R.'G REP. 237 (June 19, 2002), 2003 WL 22016895.

I did not learn humility from my family. Empathy and compassion were rarely discussed, modeled, or learned values at our dinner table. My detractors would say I have failed to break that pattern.

But my life is also blessed. I've often done and do a lot of good, too. Maybe that's what continually saves me.

---

[28] In contrast to Professor Sutherland's definition, by "white-collar," I mean something more conventional and legal: "Non-violent crime for financial gain committed by means of deception by persons whose occupational status is entrepreneurial, professional or semi-professional and utilizing their special occupational skills and opportunities; also, nonviolent crime for financial gain utilizing deception and committed by anyone having special technical and professional knowledge of business and government, irrespective of the person's occupation." See BUREAU OF JUSTICE STATISTICS, U.S. DEPARTMENT OF JUSTICE, DICTIONARY OF CRIMINAL JUSTICE DATA TERMINOLOGY 215 (2nd ed. Search Group, Inc. 1981).

For a brief and clear history of corporate crime, *see* Etzioni, Amitai. A366 Corporate Crime. International Handbook of White-Collar Crime, 2007, pp. 187-199. http://hdl.handle.net/1961/4002

Now, in my fifties, I'm starting to make sense of things. I have reflections to share that describe many felons' path to trouble, our post-conviction challenges, some thoughts about how best to make things right.

*   *

For too long, to me "no" meant only that we hadn't talked enough yet. I can still be this way, but I have better judgment about when to persist and am less certain about what I "deserve." "Because I broke the law" is far too simplistic an explanation for why and how I became disbarred with a non-sealable, non-expungeable felony.

At our worst, we white-collars are the best rationalizers, and we are the most entitled. That's why we cause so much trouble with access to money in weak or tense moments. To the extent I was a victim of anything, it was mostly of distorted self-importance, flattery and my thorough unwillingness as a young adult to delay self-gratification.

I blame no one for anything, yet try as I might to shake it, I do have my "Scarlet F": a near-permanently stigmatized identity.

Stigmatized identity is the most pernicious collateral consequence of felony and infamy.[29] All felons function within penumbras of shame, no matter who we are or to what degree. Regardless of whether any one of us is aware of our unique stigma, stigmatized identity is the singular obstacle all felons must conquer enough to move forward once convicted.[30]

---

[29] I vaguely knew what I'd been feeling, and didn't understand the stigmatic aspect of my felony until I was recently off probation and serendipitously stumbled upon the invaluable book that opened a major door for me, because it convinced me I had a future in teaching, among other things. Richards, Stephen and Jeffrey Ross. "Convict Criminology" (Wadsworth 2003).

See www.ConvictCriminology.org ("The 'New School of Convict Criminology' is a relatively new and controversial perspective in the field of corrections and the academic field of criminology. It challenges the way crime and correctional problems are traditionally represented and discussed by researchers, policymakers, and politicians.")

[30] Shame that only stigmatizes serves no one. Whereas, shame that is "reintegrative" as contemplated by restorative justice thinkers serves the common good. See, e.g., J.W. Barnard, "Reintegrative Shaming Theory in Corporate Sentencing." 79 S. Cal. L. Rev. 959-1007 (1999).

The "felon" label frequently has been a condition of my existence where I carry this attribute that discredits me as a normal person; it bestows moral impurity, invites moral judgment, and creates a severe sense of "otherness." This is my felon demon. It's not outwardly visible to others like a birth defect.

"Felony" doesn't endear one to others like someone innocently stigmatized: a wounded war veteran beyond repair, a cancer survivor, a paraplegic accident victim, or someone who is developmentally challenged.

We felons chose this, some say. Others who are stigmatized and acceptable in spite of their stigma didn't choose to break the law.

Seventeen years after committing the crimes that led to my felony conviction, I still sometimes fight not to see myself in a negative light, to be consistently open with my children and others about my criminal record, and to refrain from internalizing negative attitudes about myself. It's been hard work over the years to keep this Sword of Damocles firmly suspended to fight entropy and avoid physical, mental, emotional and spiritual decay.

In addition to my own stigma, there are "the villifiers:" people whose scripts don't work unless I'm eternally bad, which is an easy case to make for a villifier. While invoking a Chris Rock schtick one of my daughters has encouraged me to welcome the villifiers, (she calls them "haters") claiming their presence indicates I am doing something well, or correctly.

For the villifiers, my best will never be good enough or perceived as sincere and without agenda. The better an idea or more creative an approach I have to accomplishing anything, the more scrutiny I invite. Every carefully inventoried, darkly characterized, and sadly hurtful human mistake I have made since my conviction, and every mistake I will make in my nefarious future "prove" I am a lifelong criminal.

Other felons live with this same "Scarlet F". It's the aspect of felony for which to be healthy we must strive to summon St. Francis-quality equanimity.

In contrast, my post-conviction challenges of the ilk non-felons *do* commonly share are garden variety nuisances: pricey gasoline, obscene health care costs, claim-stalling insurance companies, banks that make money from everything but lending, child support obligations coupled with job lay-offs, and divorce lawyers.

I often wish these common nuisances were the rule rather than the exception, but too often the main piece of my "felon demon" predominates: the shame that I cannot reverse the harm I caused when I broke the law. I'm not misguided in wrestling this demon, but I've learned this grappling tends not to heal.

Until recently, I've wrestled the demon because due to my felony, I can likely never earn enough money to meet my personal and family obligations, be sure to educate my children respectably, *and* make good dollar-for-dollar on the financial loss my former senior law colleague, Jack, would say he sustained from my crimes.

Making good on my many post-conviction obligations is equally challenging. Life costs at least as much for felons as for non-felons. Plus, no amount of money can reverse the emotional and psychological pain I caused Jack and his wife. That reversal, sadly, might never come in their lifetimes. I'm stuck with that. But so are they, since they alone control how they heal from what happened. The same goes for my other villifiers. And so it is I've become more willing to release the felon demon.

*   *

There is another important reason I'm releasing the demon. I'm now convinced money is neither the only way I can make good, nor the only way other white-collars can make good. Money might even - at times - be a wrong way for us to make good, because it's so narrow.

We white-collars owe more than the boatloads of money we can likely never earn to make good financially. While doing my best to make good financially is *one* right thing to do, it's hardly the only right thing, because money is hardly ever a complete answer for problem solving.

Money is an intuitively appealing, handy but often ineffective tool to redress harm. Without conjuring images of tassle-loafered trial lawyers or blaming the system by which tort victims access courthouses through contingent fee arrangements, tort law inevitably under compensates many victims,[31] and falls short as a

---

[31] *See* Richard L. Abel, A Critique of Torts, 37 UCLA L. REV. 785, 797–98 (1990) (victims with extreme injuries maybe undercompensated because they need immediate funds, and sometimes settle quickly and cheaply).

restorative measure, since it can only address wrongdoing with financial compensation.[32]

The law can't unhurt hurt feelings or relieve more serious human pain. In this way, the law of civil wrongs is hollow. The criminal law can be equally impotent for crime victims and the greater community. Criminal law focuses primarily on punishing and deterring lawbreakers, and too infrequently - if ever - on healing or restoration.

In economic parlance, compensation would be "perfect" if the victim ends up "indifferent." But in real life there are no "indifferent victims."[33] So, it's a mistake of law and policy to think money alone can heal.

---

[32] RICHARD A. POSNER, ECONOMIC ANALYSIS OF LAW 25 (5th ed. 1998), at 237. (tort law requires tortfeasors to pay victims money and enjoins tortfeasors from committing future wrongs).

[33] *E.g.*, Presumably a paraplegic injured by a drunk driver would rather walk than have millions of dollars.

Making a victim truly "whole" is as subjective as determining "loss,"[34] and as imprecise as knowing with certainty when a recovering alcoholic, recovering drug addict, recovering lawyer or felon has been "rehabilitated."

There is no certainty. There are only indicia. But I am certain the main equation must be restorative. And, restoration can begin only by first examining how we got in trouble and how we can use the source of that trouble to avoid wasting a good mind with apt, empowering solutions.

*   *

---

[34] *See, e.g.*, ROBERT COOTER & THOMAS ULEN, LAW AND ECONOMICS 46, 49 (3ded. 2000) (applying economic theories to property, contract, and tort law).

I. ON PAIN

A. ENTROPY

I met a traveler from an antique land
Who said: "Two vast and trunkless legs of stone
Stand in the desert. Near them on the sand,
Half sunk, a shattered visage lies, whose frown
And wrinkled lip and sneer of cold command
Tell that its sculptor well those passions read
Which yet survive, stamped on these lifeless things,
The hand that mocked them and the heart that fed.
And on the pedestal these words appear:
`My name is Ozymandias, King of Kings:
Look on my works, ye mighty, and despair!'
Nothing beside remains. Round the decay
Of that colossal wreck, boundless and bare,
The lone and level sands stretch far away.

Ozymandias, by Percy Bysshe Shelley, 1818

The second law of thermodynamics is entropy: order naturally devolves toward chaos. That's my definition, anyway. There are several, granted. And yes, the right energy infused into the chaos-bound system can stop entropy, sometimes.

Entropy is an immutable, ubiquitous force of nature. It applies to every physical, mental, emotional, spiritual, moral and ethical circumstance, challenge, decision, and every relationship in every human being's life, and not just to greenhouses or the Universe trillions of years from now, when all that will exist is nothing wrapped in radiation.

Entropy conspires against human virtue and excellence, and is the root of human denial. It's why doing the right thing is often far more difficult than doing the wrong thing. Entropy is why Mediocrity is the Tenth Muse.

If there is evil, entropy is evil's engine. In law, entropy boldly challenges us to do more than the law requires and less than the law allows. In business, entropy dares us to leave money on the table when we can take it all, and to put more on the table than absolutely necessary.

Entropy is why free will is so complex.

Chinua Achebe wrote about entropy in "Things Fall Apart." So did Isaac Asimov in "The Last Question." Thomas Pynchon wrote about it in his readable short story, "Entropy," his amusing novella, "The Crying of Lot 49," and his brain teaser "Gravity's Rainbow," an irony of which for me is when I was collecting antiquarian books I acquired the galley proof of "Gravity's Rainbow," but had to fire sale it when I ran out of money.

Ecclesiastes 3:20: "all are of the dust, and all turn to dust again."

*   *

I left Altheimer & Gray ("A & G") in early Winter, 1991. A & G was the fancy, large law firm that trained and raised me upon graduation from law school. I left to start my own commercial litigation boutique and make real money instead of just a living. I felt the $100,000 or so which I was earning then at age 32 after four years of practice was a pittance, and that the partners would always take advantage of my 2300 billable hours annually by throwing me some vestige of the partnership spoils - unless and until I might make partner in three more years (which I had no reason to doubt). But I had no patience. I wanted much more, immediately.

One of the A & G partners said to me: "You're making a huge mistake. This will be your downfall. If you stay here, you have a stable future." I'd always thought he was pompous, and I thought so when he said that to me.

This partner was only half right. A & G later fell apart after 80 years in business. A lot of lawyers - partners, too - were left without jobs. Many lost a lot of money. Some left the firm as litigation defendants. The firm had imploded under their own weight and mismanagement. Hubris, I suspect. Entropy?

When I was practicing law, I forgot all the literature I'd read before I became a lawyer, and all those antiquarian books I was collecting (but was often too busy to read) all still applied to me. I forgot doing the right thing still mattered, despite what may be "legal." I believed too much and in a distorted way, in the law school indoctrination that teaches law students their ethical duty as lawyers lies with the client and beyond that to the court, and that discharging those duties requires zealot advocacy and application of all legal means to protect or advance the client's interests.

This indoctrination can be problematic, because while it does breed if not teach ethical relativism (at least that's how I perceived things then), it certainly does not include an exhortation to ignore normal notions of right and wrong, fair play or substantial justice. But I forgot that part.

And I'm not alone in the profession on this front, which is why so many regular people frequently despise lawyers. So many lawyers exist in the grey area and shadows of "right and wrong" as non-lawyers know that concept.

When ethical relativism is exalted as it is somewhat in law school, and becomes one's stock-in-trade in practice as it did for me, trouble brews in the soul of the ethically challenged, because to prevail entropy has so little work to do.

For me, when it came to my pocketbook and survival, keeping my moral compass pointing north was an overwhelming challenge. Yet, never for a minute (until it was way too late) did I ever consider myself a bad decision maker or still worse: a bad person. But I did enough bad things it's taken me nearly 17 years for what I feel is clear and healthy reflection.

There were key crossroads and propitious moments I ignored even if I recognized them. The first principal moment of truth and crossroad revealed itself to me in late 1994. My little law firm, of which I was principal rainmaker, was growing way too fast.

We were ridiculously under diversified, undercapitalized and mismanaged. Two thirds of our seven-figure revenue came from one client - my client. But there were at that time five to seven lawyers in the firm. That was all screwed up, and I knew it in my gut but ignored it.

I did tell Jack I needed help running the firm. He balked. He reminded me of our agreement when we began practicing law together: he wanted no part of day-to-day management. (Neither of us, I don't think, foresaw our rapid growth.) Still, that was a pretty Faustian deal for us both; Jack really wasn't free to make that buck-passing deal as far as the law of law office management is concerned. We are indeed our brothers' keepers. Yet, Jack said when he'd been growing his law firm with his father, his father always insisted he have his hand on the rudder; I should do the same; that there was no justification otherwise. And, I capitulated.

Damned entropy.

Trusting one's instincts and doing the right thing can be so difficult. Doing the smart and necessary thing, and standing up for oneself, is too. This was a key moment in time that, with hindsight, I should have told Jack, who worked half-time at best and wintered elsewhere, that without proper, business-like financial controls I would rather fold tent, return to a large firm, go back on a salary and make less money working for other partners who might pay me my "due."

At this point, my annual personal and family overhead was around $300,000. I had a mortgaged house in Glencoe, a closet full of handmade suits and other very expensive clothing, a wife and two young daughters. When things were "stable," we had a housekeeper and a nanny at all times (13 of them, if I remember correctly). Most if not all were illegal immigrants whom we paid in cash. We had two health club memberships, two personal trainers, Pilates classes, high real estate taxes, private school tuitions, ski trips to our second residence in Colorado, several Mercedes, a BMW, a Saab, and so on. I "needed" every penny of the money I was taking out of the firm – right under Jack's nose.

So, I drew on my crown prince upbringing, and the myths I was raised to believe in about myself: I was without admitting it a legal version of Tom Wolfe's "Master of the Universe" in Bonfires of the Vanities. I convinced myself I could succeed with huge results. Since I was already successful at marketing my firm, I would simply continue to do so and become even more proficient. I would land bigger and better clients with even bigger and better cases. Sooner than later I would convince Jack I needed a lot of help and someone more experienced in business management to run this business like a business, and not like a fraternity with an over-empowered, entitled and self-important bantam rooster at the helm.

But I hid my fear with arrogance. I didn't say what was really bothering and frightening me: I was overwhelmed with my roles as chief cook and bottle washer. I had little effective mentoring. I was concerned if I was left to handle everything by myself (hiring, firing, marketing, lawyering, and office management) this would compromise my ability to do what I did best: attract clients and steward their cases to settlements, so we would get paid and then as rapidly as possible move on to the next client. I was yearning for some help to solve the lawyer's plague: a mule can't reproduce itself and you're only as good as your last client.

Also, I knew I was always paying myself too much money, but there was no one to stop me. I kept my mouth shut until about four months later when the next propitious moment emerged.

This time, the issue was an externality beyond our control, but as to which we could certainly control our response. It behooved us to do something smart then, but we did not. We continued to wear our "Masters of the Universe" blindfolds.

In late Winter or early Spring 1995, I learned we had a viability risk with our biggest client, i.e., the client who was sometimes paying us $20,000 - $60,000 weekly. I learned from a friend inside this client the company was "in play." A turnaround specialist had been retained. The old but "friendly" President would get the boot, and with the new turnaround specialist would come a new in-house General Counsel who was reputed to be a penny-pinching, fly-specking, anti-law firm hatchet man for management.

I'm simplifying matters, but not much. Our response was to try to weather the brewing storm on the presumptuous notion our good legal work would be recognized and rewarded no matter who ran the client's company. What fools we were. Looking back, we should have taken sober stock, closed the firm, gone to work elsewhere, and let the chips fall where they might have fallen with that client and our futures. Instead, we moved forward motivated by our greedy pipe dream and plagued by entropy. We didn't know the party would be over, and there would be no way when the client relationship collapsed and our fees evaporated that we could quickly enough get more clients or more partners with more clients.

There would be no riches or security for our little law firm. To this point in my life I never would have said I was the least bit superstitious, but I became so after listening to an eerie voice mail message.

While our biggest client was going south on us, I was also concluding representation of former Wall Street Journal "Heard on the Street" columnist, Robert T. "Tim" Metz.

Several years earlier, Tim had been fleeced by a crooked investment advisor, Scott Serfling, whom Tim had profiled in his book "Black Monday - The Stock Market Catastrophe of October 19, 1987." After many years, I had managed to find Serfling, but only a bit of Tim's money. I had worked with the FBI to bring Serfling to justice.

My office was in the Marquette Building, across from the federal court. I'd returned minutes after Serfling's sentencing hearing, at which he was taken into custody and carted off to prison.

As I left the courtroom, Serfling's girlfriend called me a prick and spit in my face. I wiped it off and left. I did a few things once back in my office and then listened to my voice mail messages. There was a frightening voice mail message from a woman whom I'm still pretty sure was Serfling's girlfriend, the spitter.

"You motherfucker. You better watch yourself carefully. You better sleep with one eye open. You have no idea what kind of ride you are in for. It'll be a shit storm like you can't imagine. You are so smug in your classy suits, expensive shoes, and that fancy leather briefcase of yours. You just couldn't leave well enough alone, could you? Well you better hold on, pal, cause' here it comes."

I thought this was related to Serfling. I called the Glencoe police. They had a car watch my house for a few days, until it seemed a non-issue; like a harmless, barking dog. I told everyone at the firm about it. Everyone shrugged their shoulders and pressed on.

I didn't know it then, nor did Jack know it. But this spooky prophecy was the last missed crossroad after which I would then face enough stress that I moved from the pressures of resisting entropy to the temptation and consequence of felony and infamy.

*   *

B. **FELONY AND INFAMY**

I N - FA - M Y[35]

1. Extremely bad reputation, public reproach, or strong condemnation as the result of a shameful, criminal, or outrageous act: a time that will live in infamy.

2. Infamous character or conduct.

3. An infamous act or circumstance.

4. Law. Loss of rights, incurred by conviction of an infamous offense.

   Synonyms: disrepute,   obloquy,   odium, opprobrium, shame. See disgrace.

   Antonyms: credit, honor.

   Infamy[36]   (Latin *in*, not, and *fama*, fame.) Infamy is loss of a good name. When this has been brought about by regular legal process, terminating in a conviction in a court of justice, no injury is done to the criminal by publishing the fact. . . . It is twofold in species, infamy of law (*infamia juris*) and infamy of fact (*infamia facti*).

---

[35] http://dictionary.reference.com/browse/infamy

[36]   Delany,   Joseph.   "Infamy."   The   Catholic Encyclopedia. Vol. 8. New York: Robert Appleton Company,   1910.   19   Jan.   2010 http://www.newadvent.org/cathen/08001a.htm

Infamy of law is contracted in one of three ways. Either the law itself attaches this juridical ineligibility and incapacity to the commission of certain crimes, or makes it contingent upon the decision of a judge, or finally connects it with the penalty imposed by him. . . .

Infamy of fact is the result of a widespread opinion, by which the community attributes some unusually serious delinquency, such as adultery or the like, to a person. This is more of an unfitness than an irregularity properly so called, unless sentence in court has been pronounced.

It ceases therefore when one has shown by a change of life extending over a period of two or probably three years that his repentance is sincere.

*   *

A common oxymoron that non-felons and even some felons use is the term "ex-felon." No felon is ever an "ex-felon" absent a pardon, and even pardons don't always operate as expungements or sealings.[37] My longing desire to become anonymously conventional, i.e., a non-felon, will likely remain a dream.

---

[37] A pardon is public forgiveness from a state Governor (for state offenses) or the President of the United States (for federal offenses).

There will likely always be that question on nearly every job application: "Have you ever been convicted of a felony and if so, please explain."

Let me explain:

The first day I practiced law was in late August 1986. I went to the bathroom and a very elderly, senior member of the firm parked himself at the urinal beside me. He turned his head toward me and asked:

"Are you one of the new kids?"

I said "yes."

He asked: "Do you want the best advice anyone could ever give you in this profession?"

I smiled and nodded, amused by the awkward circumstance. Leaning over while doing his urinal business, as if somehow someone might hear what he would say, he attempted to whisper but said somewhat loudly:

"Your worst enemy in this business is always your biggest client. There's nothing your biggest client can't do for you or to you."

I smiled and thanked him. We finished our business. He died a week later, and I never thought about what he said to me until it was too late.

When my oldest daughter was about 6 years old, she asked me, "Daddy, what exactly do you do for your clients?" I answered her honestly and without hesitation, "I help rich people get and keep money."

A versatile attorney friend of mine, who had a substantial criminal defense practice but with whom I periodically co-counseled commercial cases, once asked me: "How can you represent these businessmen day in and day out? I don't know how you do it."

"What are you talking about?," I asked. "You routinely defend murderers and rapists."

"Yes. Exactly. With them it's usually straightforward. They either did it or they didn't, but with these business clients you never really know what the hell is going on."

*   *

In 1952, Ernest Hemingway published "The Old Man and the Sea," about the Cuban fisherman who hadn't caught a fish for 84 days. He finally hooks an enormous Marlin, kills it, lashes it along side his boat, but before he gets to shore in the morning, despite his arduous battles with the sharks throughout the night, the sharks have bitten off all the meat and the fisherman is left with a skeleton.

In my law practice I wanted to be a smart fisherman, not arguably, foolish like Hemingway's hero. From my big fish when I hooked them, I was more prone to hack off the best chunks of meat and put them in the bottom of my boat leaving only the carcass for the sharks.

In Kurt Vonnegut's "God Bless You, Mr. Rosewater," there is Fred Rosewater, not unlike a Willy Loman. Fred is a bored life insurance salesman whose wife befriends a rich lesbian to consume some of her rich friend's "golden crumbs." And there is a lawyer in this novel who concocts a grand scheme to declare Eliot Rosewater, president of another branch of the rich Rosewater Family Foundation insane, so he can get the foundation's money and digest a few golden crumbs of his own.

In the second half of my career, having abhorred too many bosses and the rigid hourly fee at A & G, I started my own firm and worked largely on contingent fees or hybrid fee arrangements in high stakes commercial litigation. I was routinely trolling for Marlin or catching golden crumbs.

In my law practice, if I wasn't catching Marlin and protecting them from the sharks, I knew I had to be a golden crumbs guy. I well understood that in private commercial practice, the lawyer is never as rich as his or her richest client.

The lawyer is merely a cost of doing business. And, importantly, every time a large chunk of money changes hands, golden crumbs do fall off. So, as a lawyer with an entrepreneurial commercial litigation practice, I had to make the golden crumbs fall and catch those crumbs when they fell. But, while I caught them as often as possible, I consumed them voraciously and shared them unfairly with most of the lawyers in my firm who helped create and earn them.

Essentially, I was excellent at dispassionately valuing and monetizing a dispute. I used commercial litigation and alternative dispute resolution (arbitration and mediation) as vehicles through which I could maneuver and position disputing parties to settle, so that a larger chunk of money would change hands upon consummation of a settlement; I could either hack off the best chunks of meat or would be paid my golden crumbs. I usually did so by exposing their own weaknesses to invariably marginally honest adverse parties who were always fighting over the same thing: money.

Ironically, the case mostly at the core of my undoing and the firm's failure, was not resolved by settlement, but by an arbitrator after almost three years and 10,000 man hours of hard fought litigation.[38]

To set the stage, I will first provide a shorter overview of this disaster, followed by a more detailed version:

For our boutique litigation firm, this case had been our 84 days without catching a fish. We had this case on a "hybrid" fee basis. We agreed to charge the client reduced hourly fees of only $140 per hour no matter the relative experience of the lawyers who would work on the case, together with what came later: a "kicker" of 20% of any recovery. At 10,000 man-hours at $140 hourly,

---

[38] For perspective, 10,000 hours in our type of law practice was the rough equivalent of four lawyers working 25% of their time on this case for three years.

over three years of litigation, we had been paid a handful over $1,000,000 before the arbitrator ruled. That might sound like a lot of money, but with many hands on deck over three years, it's not that much money; not when you are paying high overhead and feeding families.

An added problem with our fee arrangement: the 20% kicker was added to the mix after the client got sick of paying hourly fees and frankly, after we were more sure we'd win than lose.

Under applicable law, a mid-stream change of fee arrangement with a client is generally considered presumptively fraudulent and to the client's disadvantage, even if the client requests the change, as our client did.[39] The changed arrangement is presumed fraudulent, not *per se* (by itself) fraudulent.

---

[39] Franciscan Sisters Health Care Corp. v. Dean, 448 N.E.2d 872 (Ill. 1983) (presumption of undue influence arises when lawyers enter into any transaction with a client during a fiduciary relationship.); In re Marriage of Pagano, 607 N.E.2d 1242, 1247 (Ill. 1992) (When lawyers enter into a new fee agreement after the lawyer has been retained, it is presumed the lawyer exercised undue influence.) *See also* American Home Assurance Co. v. Golomb, 606 N.E.2d 793, 795 (Ill. App. 4th Dist. 1992).

So, if there is ever a fee dispute, the circumstances for the changed arrangement will be scrutinized with the onus on the lawyer to "burst the bubble" of the fraudulent presumption.

The lawyer must prove there was in fact no fraud and further, regardless of whether the client requested the change, the change was to the client's advantage and in the client's best interest.[40]

The rationale for this presumption is as fiduciaries, lawyers are bound with a fiduciary duty that among other things prevents putting the lawyer's interests ahead of the client's interest.

---

[40] To rebut the presumption of undue influence, the lawyer must present evidence that he or she made a full and fair disclosure to the client of all material facts, the client's agreement was based on adequate consideration, the client had independent advice before completing the transaction and the transaction is fair. See Neville v. Davinroy, 355 N.E.2d 86, 88-89 (Ill. App. 5th Dist. 1976) (lawyer rebutted presumption of undue influence where client understood she was ultimately responsible for attorneys fees and, therefore, did not need independent legal advice).

The legal logic and conventional wisdom goes something like this: if the lawyer changes the fee arrangement to his advantage after the lawyer has reliable insight into the outcome of the case, such that the lawyer will make more money than without the change, then it's presumably to the client's disadvantage.

That logic holds and sometimes this result obtains, usually when the facts are akin to a lawyer with the proverbial widow or orphan client, and the lawyer simply uses his superior position and knowledge to make more money by overreaching and essentially forcing a unilateral change of terms on the client.

This was hardly our case. We never gave a moment's thought to whether the circumstances that presented us with a changed fee arrangement remotely resembled a presumptively or actually fraudulent situation.

This sophisticated corporate client's finances had become highly challenged since we had taken on this case. They had paid us over $1 million over the three-year life of the case: approximately $25-$30,000 monthly. They were also paying our firm at least an additional $25,000-$30,000 monthly on other litigation matters.

In the case in which we changed the fee agreement, at some point I don't remember precisely, the client through its own in-house General Counsel and President approached us and asked if we would agree to change from reduced hourly fees of $140 to 20% of the recovery. We agreed.

Months later, the arbitrator's subsequent award was $6.64 million, but ultimately the sharks left us with nothing but a skeleton and not even a few golden crumbs, despite that I had upon entry of this award, paid $5,000 to a top New York investigator who found the money to satisfy the arbitrator's award parked in a Bermuda bank.

We brought this money in Bermuda to the attention of the federal judge before whom we had initially filed the case and before whom we had confirmed the arbitration award.[41] The judge prevailed upon opposing counsel, who had been

---

[41] Both sides in this dispute had initially filed their claims and counterclaims as a lawsuit in US District Court, but the parties later both agreed to arbitrate the case based on arbitration provisions in the disputed contracts. When this occurs, the initial federal judge retains jurisidiction over the case during and after the arbitration. It then becomes the province of that federal judge to confirm, i.e., memorialize, the arbitrator's award so it becomes for all purposes a federal court judgment akin to a judgment entered in any other lawsuit.

this judge's law clerk earlier in his career, to move the cash to Chicago and to deposit $6.64 million with the Clerk of the District Court.   But ultimately that didn't matter.

There ultimately ensued a disastrous fight over our 20% fee. When the time came, the client with its new General Counsel refused to pay us. He claimed we'd been paid "enough."

The new General Counsel "relied" on a line of Illinois cases which hold that a client's "excessive fee" defense against an attorney - despite the terms of any agreement - was a summary judgment proof fact question for a jury or judge.[42] This of course means the lawyer can't

---

[42] McCracken & McCracken, P.C. v. Haegele, 618 N.E.2d 577, 581-82 (Ill. App. 4th Dist. 1993); In re Doyle, 581 N.E.2d 669, 674 (Ill. 1991); In re Teichner, 470 N.E.2d 972 (Ill. 1984); In re Marriage of Pagano, 607 N.E.2d 1242, 1249-50 (Ill. 1993). In Maksym v. Loesch, 937 F.2d 1237 (7th Cir. 1991), a lawyer sued his client to recover on a contract for attorneys' fees. The client raised an excessive fee defense and claimed the lawyer had violated of Illinois Code of Professional Responsibility Rule 2-106 (factors that determine when attorney's fees are reasonable). The Court of Appeals for the Seventh Circuit, applying Illinois law, found that a contract for professional services can be rendered unenforceable if found contrary to public policy. The Court stated that although not every violation of the rules of professional ethics will make a lawyer's contract with his client voidable *per se*, "conduct which violates both professional ethics and contract law, such as the charging of exorbitant fees

just point to the fee agreement and say: "Hey, Judge, no trial is needed. We win because the client agreed to this. The contract says so."

The problem for us from a legal standpoint was the facts of those cases upon which the new General Counsel "relied" involved situations where an attorney overreached a little old lady for doing very little on her behalf, or where the fees charged were for one reason or another outrageous, and usually in some gross disproportion to what was at stake.

The difference in all these cases was salient, to us. Our case involved a long-time, well informed, sophisticated corporate client that had been represented by in-house counsel every step of the way in nothing but arm's length dealings with our law firm.

To make it worse, this cagey client fully appreciated our practical predicament when the new General Counsel said to me:

---

by a lawyer, is not placed beyond the reach of contract law because it violates professional standards as well." Maksym, 937 F.2d at 1244. I discuss this case again *infra*, at 120.

"Go ahead and sue. I can just see it: the ungrateful Jew boy telling the 'South Side jury' you deserve over $1 million after you've already been paid over $1 million dollars."[43]

So, there is an essential ingredient for my downfall; it was this seven-figure fee dispute with our biggest client. This client that requested the changed fee arrangement was a subsidiary of a public company the Chairman of the Board of which was a former presidential cabinet member. The spouse of a U.S. Senator owned or controlled a huge stake in this company.

I had represented this client for my entire career, beginning almost immediately when I graduated from law school in 1986, when I was 27. They had made my career. They had made my law firm. Because of this one client, by the time I was 35, my annual income taxes exceeded what I had been earning annually at A & G. There was nothing this client hadn't done for me or couldn't do to me.

---

[43] For readers who might not fully appreciate this ugly remark, it's a hideous ethnic and racial slur at both me and at what in Chicago could have been a predominantly African-American jury. Among other things, this remark plays on historic tension between the Jewish and African-American communities, and signals this new General Counsel's willingness to use that to renege and lever a better deal for a lot of money.

*   *

And so it was I was "the ungrateful Jew boy."
What follows are the details of how I ended up
disbarred on consent for major trust account
violations, and a felony conviction for theft:

The funds of this client - our biggest client -
which I allowed to be taken from our trust
account, i.e., the money that is the subject of my
felony conviction, over time exceeded $500,000.
This was from the trust account into which this
client's friendly General Counsel had placed
$725,000.

At the time of this deposit, the friendly General
Counsel told me not only why they wanted to
change the fee arrangement as I have described
previously, but also that they wanted to use that
money (someone else's money, as I will explain)
to pay us for this huge case. Even at $140 hourly
our fees had over the three-year life of this case
exceeded their legal budget. And, importantly,
they also wanted to use our trust account to
shelter money away from creditors given a
looming insolvency and possible bankruptcy.

I hadn't known until the issue of where to deposit
the money surfaced, the client had long lied about
this $725,000 to the Securities and Exchange
Commission ("SEC") and to their shareholders;
they had reported to the SEC that these funds

allegedly had years earlier been paid to whom they were owed.

That was false.

The client had put this money in a separate bank account in a bank different than the bank that held all its other accounts, and never had paid the creditor.

When the client foresaw a bankruptcy, and the possibility they would have to list these funds on bankruptcy schedules as funds the client had in its possession, the client recognized the gross inconsistency with the SEC filings in which they had falsely claimed these funds had already been paid to the creditor.

When the client, through the friendly General Counsel, asked me about this inconsistency, the ensuing discussion led to the idea of depositing this $725,000 in our client trust account, so our firm and the client could say those funds were earmarked for our fees.

Basically, in acquiescing with the carrot of a presumably sure source of money ultimately going to us, I was probably assisting this client in laying the foundation for bankruptcy fraud and assisting the client in continuing to mislead its shareholders and the SEC.

The bottom line: the money we were taking into our trust account didn't rightfully belong to the client, but rather to that client's creditor. The creditor to whom the client owed this $725,000 was, conveniently, the adverse party in the biggest piece of litigation (the three-year arbitration I've referenced above) my client had ever had, my law firm had ever had, and the biggest, most complex case of my career.

Simply, my client knew damn well they owed the adverse party in this case $725,000 from a different deal. They figured if we won, their opponent – the adverse creditor - would owe them more as a result of our successful damage claim, and the $725,000 would be a set-off. It turned out they were right. But legally, they were resorting to "self-help," which while practical, is not a legal remedy. But it was the tactic we recommended to the client.

Even now, I don't know if Jack seriously considered this at the time. I know I never discussed the source of this $725,000 with him thoroughly. He knew the client wanted to keep the money from a creditor.

But that was our job: helping rich people get money and keep money, and catching big golden crumbs or catching big fish and hacking off big chunks of meat.

I told Jack maybe twice the money was falsely reported to the SEC, had been shown as paid, and had long been off the client's books. Apart from whether Jack had his own duty to inquire further once I indicated the source of these funds, I never pressed to ensure he properly focused on this. I didn't want him to focus. I knew how very dirty this money was when we accepted the deposit by wire to our trust account in May of 1995.

We viewed those funds essentially as the best security we could get for payment of hundreds of thousands of dollars, if not more than a million dollars, we were almost certain this client would owe us several months later.

We took these funds when the then-friendly General Counsel told me not only was the company in trouble and had hired a turn-around specialist to fix it, but it was a near certainty this General Counsel would soon be fired together with the company President. Soon, we were warned, there would likely be no one inside this client who would be an ally of our law firm.

The elephant in the room: this client was fully capable of stiffing us, too. After all, on our advice this client was thrilled to resort to self-help on holding back $725,000, which they knew they owed to the creditor whom we were suing about something else, and about which they had long before we ever weighed in lied repeatedly to the SEC and their shareholders. We had to figure with a turn-around guy coming in with whom we had no relationship and no history, they were fully capable of using our own self-help strategy against us if money was tight. And we clearly knew their money was tight.

So, we accepted that $725,000 rationalizing - in some crude, twisted way - that "possession is 9/10's of the law." Of course, in hindsight, we should have refused the money. I should have gone out of my way to make sure Jack fully appreciated where this money came from. I wish I had. Most likely, it would not have been there for me to misuse before we were entitled to it, because I believe if Jack had fully appreciated the source of that $725,000, given that he was 35 years senior to me and since maybe his moral compass was not as impaired as mine, he would never have allowed us to put that $725,000 into our trust account. He likely would have - as he taught us to do for our clients − lived with the bad facts we had been dealt and worked around them.

My prophetic, friendly General Counsel was right. This lawyer and the friendly President were fired not long after they gave us the $725,000, and a handful of time before we would receive word from the arbitrator that we had won this client $6.64 million.

When we received their $725,000, Jack and I were confident the arbitrator would rule in our favor on the strength of our liability case. We were equally confident the money damages to which our client would be entitled would be in the multiple millions based on the evidence. With that kind of victory in the offing, twenty percent (20%) of these funds was supposed to go to our firm. But in all candor, we didn't know. Pigs fly in courtrooms.

Still, in my view at the time, our assessment of the likely outcome meant if we won all we suspected we would win, then net of the $725,000 we were already holding, the client would still owe us over half a million dollars.

But then came the attack of brutal economic terrorism. The new General Counsel, whom I viewed then and still do view as a gangster with a law license, called me and told me – in the first conversation I'd ever had with him – they would be slowing payment on all our cases while they audited all our firm's billings on the many pieces of litigation we had handled and were handling for them. He claimed the turnaround team "believed" we had "hornswoggled" the prior General Counsel and President into believing litigation had been the best way to resolve many of their legal problems.

How sophisticated lawyers and corporate executives operating at arms' length "hornswoggle" one another as to how best to resolve disputes was always beyond me, and I still find the assertion galling. But that's what he said. He also said they would not pull their cases from us, but going forward and during their "audit" of our billings, "so as not to compromise our legal positions" in any of their cases, they expected us to continue representing them, given their "belief" when we had represented them on the defense side of things, or when we had billed them hourly, we had padded our billings and, in regular parlance, ripped them off over many years "possibly for hundreds of thousands if not millions of dollars."

Translation: they didn't want to incur the inefficiencies of changing counsel midstream or to reveal to new counsel they were stiffing prior counsel. They just wanted something for nothing from us while they postured to chisel us on our fees.

The new General Counsel's claims were cut from whole cloth. But frankly, any law firm that represents one client for many years on many cases can be vulnerable to this sort of claim just from the sheer volume of transactions, time entries, suboptimal detail or arguable vagueness of the time descriptions, the faxes, photocopies, conferences, meetings, depositions, and so on.

So there we were in the crosshairs of our major client; terribly undiversified in our client base and now confronting significant cash flow challenges. My awful response was for the rest of that year (about 6 months) to run the firm from the client trust account, which is off limits and which contained money we were holding for our fees, but which had not yet been fully earned, or for which we had not yet obtained proper permission from the client to transfer to our operating account.

Until I told Jack about this in late 1995, he never knew any trust account funds were used improperly. But that is because he wasn't looking and I knew he wasn't looking. I was waiting for the arbitration award and our predicted large 20% fee to sort it out and put this nightmare behind us. That 20% was how I intended to stop running out of Peters.

About the arbitration, we were right and wrong. As I said, we won the arbitration award of $6.64 million, and we collected the money, too. And, after we collected all that money and it was safely in the hands of the U.S. District Court clerk, we promptly sent this miscreant client a bill for our 20% share: $1.325 million.

To me, this client's subsequent refusal to pay us our 20%, together with their new General Counsel's assertion of the "excessive fee" and "ungrateful Jew boy" defense was evil. The client's legal position was untenable but their strategy was perfect. At this time, there were about 80,000 pending cases on any given day in the Circuit Court of Cook County, which was and remains the largest unified court system in the world. Getting that case to trial were we to sue for our fee (which we ultimately did) would have taken three to five years. And there I was, having dipped pretty far into $725,000.

To buy time, I had the nerve or chutzpah to assert a common law possessory retaining lien on the trust account due to the client's unsatisfied debt to us of $1.325 million.[44]

---

[44] At common law, i.e., based on decisions from courts and not based on statutes, lawyers can hold on to, i.e., "retain" the property of clients that is already in their possession when the client owes them money. In legalese, this is a common law possessory retaining lien. The chutzpah to which I refer is that I was asserting a possessory lien against funds in an account much of which I'd already spent; but the client didn't know that.

I then told Jack more than half these funds had been used to run the firm, and we were in big trouble. I also told a devious, heinous whopper of a lie about how it was we had used client funds. I told Jack the office manager did it, which was technically true. He knew she had check signing authority on the trust account.

I "speculated" perhaps a long time ago she had taken money and had - without my knowledge – been paying the firm's operating expenses from client funds so no one would know there were any problems. The fact is when she did that once, I let her do it more. I told this lie to save my butt if I could. And I knew it could give Jack some unspoken and oblique cover.

In Illinois, the rules of professional conduct require a lawyer who acquires information indicating another lawyer has engaged in dishonesty or misconduct, to report the wrongdoing lawyer to the Illinois Attorney Registration and Disciplinary Commission

("ARDC") or risk discipline, and possibly lose his or her own law license.[45]

Without the cover of blaming the office manager, Jack surely would have been forced to report me and, in essence, himself for having his head in the sand, not jointly having his hand on the rudder, and for allowing me to do what I had done. Lawyers who are both signatories on the same trust account do, after all, have joint fiduciary duties to clients - certainly when it comes to custody and proper disbursement of client funds.

---

[45] The rule derives from In re Himmel, 125 Ill. 531, 533 N.E.2d 790 (Ill. 1988). This is the first case in which the Illinois Supreme Court upheld the one-year suspension of a lawyer's law license for failing to report misconduct by another attorney. Attorney Himmel had reached a settlement agreement with Casey, his client's prior lawyer, for Casey's misappropriation of the client's funds rather than reporting Casey to the Illinois ARDC. Maybe the ugliest piece of the Supreme Court's Himmel decision is that the settlement Himmel negotiated for his client was arguably the best result for his client and was actually instigated by her request - and had Himmel reported the prior wrongdoing lawyer such a report might have hindered or interfered with the client's ability to recover from Casey.

Also, with the cover of blaming the office manager, I would be in a position to remain - I hoped - still practicing law and while in the hot seat with Jack, we would both be off the radar of the ARDC.

Of course, I needed the complicity of the office manager. She was a young woman in her early thirties. I wondered if she had an arguable substance abuse problem I had long ignored. I sat her down, explained the mess with Jack and the position the firm was in with the client. I explained the position Jack and I could be in with the ARDC.

I told her I was more certain than a hunch Jack would restore the client trust funds to the extent I could not, to keep the mess quiet. I told her I had to blame it on her otherwise Jack would be obligated to report me and in essence, himself, to the ARDC.

I suggested quitting with a good reference. It would be far preferable to getting kicked out anyway, because she had been signing trust account checks, albeit with my knowledge; but she had signed almost all of them.

Finally, I told her in addition to writing her a useful letter of recommendation, I suspected whether he ever would admit it, Jack would perceive me blaming her for what it was (a lie, useful for cover), and were I to suggest it, I speculated he would be amenable to paying her a severance with the unstated understanding she would keep quiet and take the blame. She went along. She got her severance.

We hired counsel, who interviewed her. She stuck to the story and took the blame. When asked why she had used the client fund account rather than an operating account, she said she didn't see those funds were not ours, since the client gave us the money as security for our fees – which is what I had told her when we accepted the funds. That was no answer in terms of right and wrong, but as I'd surmised they would, our lawyer and Jack decided to keep the matter quiet and did not report it to the ARDC.

Our lawyer, obviously, advised us to restore the account, return the money to the client or get the client to put the money in a joint escrow, and sue them. In business, that would never have happened. Business people who do not have law licenses usually do not give money back to people who owe them far more than they are holding.

Had we not been lawyers, possession likely would have been 9/10's of the law. Prime ironic example: this very client who owed our adverse party $725,000 which they refused to turn over, correctly figured the guy they were suing would end up owing them a lot more.

So, primarily Jack and to the extent I could, we restored the funds. Jack put in the vast majority of the money: about $450,000. And we didn't actually release $725,000 directly to the client. We negotiated an escrow of these funds, together with an additional $600,000 from the account of the U.S. District Court Clerk, who was holding the $6.64 million that our client was chomping at the bit to get their hands on.

With $1.325 million properly in escrow, we sued the client and ultimately settled for a lot less than we were owed.

We really couldn't afford to litigate whether our fees had been excessive over the years or in that case. We couldn't afford to earn our money twice while I was at the same time expected to rebuild the firm and repay Jack. But, the firm never recovered from the loss of that client. As I said, we were terribly under-diversified. I just could not rebuild that revenue stream and cover our overhead.

With and because of that one huge client, and until we got in this manufactured, transparent dispute with them, we had been grossing about $40,000 weekly for several years, i.e., roughly $2 million annually. Our fancy office rent was $175,000 annually for 10,000 square feet in the Loop. Our monthly payroll was in the healthy five figures. Without that client, we were in the red, and dead.

After the restoration of the trust account money in late 1995, we limped along as a firm for almost two years. But there was no way to rebuild our client base or cash flow to meet our overhead and make us a living, let alone make any real money. We were blind in entropy's glare. We should have closed the firm in 1995 when the client put us in their crosshairs.

In the aftermath of this major financial setback with our largest client, I was still practicing law and should have learned my lessons. Minimally, I should have learned how to ask for and demand help when needed. But I was far more compromised than I knew from the continuing financial stress of trying to rebuild the firm. In this entropy-tainted time, I would commit additional violations that would later become of record in the Illinois Supreme Court's ARDC by the time I turned myself in to the Cook County State's Attorney two years later.

My coping skills and judgment were a mess. My moral compass had no North. I could have been indicted for more than I was and more than I admitted. (On request, I will provide any reader with Jack's detailed affidavit. See page 229.)

Ultimately, in late Spring 1997, Jack understandably became so exasperated with my crimes that he felt he was left with little choice but to close the firm. He also told me if I didn't go to my family and get him $500,000, he would turn me in to the authorities.

At a subsequent and hastily convened meeting with Jack and a friend who is also a skilled lawyer with heart, who was helping me in these horridly dire moments, we told Jack he wasn't in business with my family; I would not ask them to give him a penny, and he was a textbook case for being the cause of his own loss. That took nerves of steel to say to him, but my lawyer friend did it with aplomb.

He also laid out for Jack other problems Jack hadn't known about; for example: back in 1995, rather than tell my wife what was really going on in the law firm, I had signed her name to the junior mortgage Jack had demanded from me on my Glencoe house as ostensible security for the $450,000 he used to right the earlier trust account mess.

That junior mortgage put the house so far under water when I signed my wife's name, with "stinkin' thinkin'" I figured it made no difference, so why bother telling her then.

Similarly, when the firm had become so financially infirm in late 1995, we had fallen behind on the $16,000 per month rent for our 10,000 square foot office.

At some point after we resolved the trust account mess, without telling Jack and to keep the landlord wolf away from the door, I negotiated a lease modification for which I needed Jack's signature, and which purported to convert the lease from one initially secured only by the firm's assets, to one that we now guaranteed personally.

I signed Jack's name and never told him about the lease extension, until that day in Spring 1997 when my lawyer friend told him about it and about other aspects of this horrendous mess, which now weighed on Jack to clean up.

One of Jack's responses was to pay the firm's creditors and most of our credit lines with the banks (for which I alone and not he had been asked to sign). He also claimed he had actually never been my partner (despite, minimally, how we had always treated and portrayed the relationship internally and to the world). His interesting theory: there was no written partnership agreement; he had merely rented his name to me).

While claiming he wasn't and had never been my partner, Jack also sent lawyers into my soon-to-follow divorce case arguing he was solely entitled to a $350,000 fee in a high profile case which "the firm" had earned during the pendency of my divorce, and which both my divorce lawyer and my wife's divorce lawyer were understandably arguing was at least presumptively marital property subject to Jack's claims – which if he were not a partner could only be based on *quantum meruit* (the value of the work he had done on that case, which exceeded barely more than taking one deposition).

The divorce court agreed the fee was presumptively marital property, and ordered the $350,000 fee escrowed subject to resolution. I waived an interest in the fee to avoid income tax liability. Jack got 90% and my wife got 10% for the benefit of my daughters – a "gift" to my daughters "from" Jack, which had no gift tax implications for him.

*   *

I must make a few things crystal clear here so no one can say I have obfuscated:

(i) Our firm was so undercapitalized I continued several times after Jack's restoration of the 1995 trust account problem to misuse other trust account funds trying to keep things afloat, i.e., I was borrowing from Peter to pay Paul while trying to rebuild our revenues.[46] That's a nice way of saying I was engaged in knowing misappropriation.

(ii) When Jack demanded $500,000 from my family and said he would keep quiet if paid, I recognized Jack's money mattered far more to him than my crimes. He put it simply: if I were to pay him the $500,000, he was fully prepared to ignore the ARDC rules for reporting fellow lawyer dishonesty.

(iii) No client in my case was the ultimate "victim," but at least in Illinois (but not in all states) that's legally irrelevant as to my culpability for my misdeeds. Also, the notion of victim here is somewhat grey. Legally, under Illinois law a crime victim is not the colleague of a lawyer who does bad things to others and maybe not even as between partners. Generally, that's what law and other firms are all about. Businesses fail.

---

[46] This is of record with the Illinois ARDC.

If there were victims, they were among my other law colleagues. I let health and malpractice insurance premiums lapse without saying so. And there were of my doing unfunded retirement payments because even before the major dispute with our biggest client I was running the firm like a pig and was never held accountable – not even by the colleague whose payments went and remain unfunded.

In a sense another victim was one of my oldest friends who also practiced in our firm. We had a lifelong relationship that extended and still does extend far beyond our careers. But when we practiced together, he deserved far more personal and financial credit for some of the big fish we caught due to his client-trolling successes, but Jack pretty much hogged the credit and best cuts of meat on these fish, and I let it happen. Pigs get fat and hogs get slaughtered.

Whether Jack and his wife were the ultimate victims, legally, is different. The bulk of the money to clean up the messes so there were no external victims came from Jack and his wife. After Jack was fully on notice of my character flaws and moral lack of center (in 1995), he still left me in nearly sole control and at the helm of what had become a sinking vessel too weak to catch enough, and ultimately, any more big fish.

Jack knew what he knew.

I never had proper management oversight, guidance or support in the firm, and I was not trained or equipped to provide that for us. I made stupid expenditures on personnel we didn't need, and on other unnecessary "wants," not needs. While it's no excuse for my moral and legal culpability, the lack of senior oversight is the precise reason I was never incarcerated.

At my sentencing hearing, the judge asked me if I had anything to say. I apologized to Jack and his wife. I told the judge how embarrassed I was to appear before him in that context. I told him if he would not incarcerate me I would endeavor to become the leader I had been trained to be, and hoped I could be judged ultimately based on my future and not simply upon how I had made such a big mess of my life and the lives of many others.

The judge paused. Then he looked squarely at Jack and his wife, who were presenting themselves as victims. He said with an extended arm and a pointed, wagging finger: "I'm not incarcerating this man. He didn't set out to cause you or anyone else harm. There was a big business snowball rolling down the hill and he was left alone to push it back up by himself."

Despite the judge's remarks, 11 years I later told the Chicago Tribune a main reason I was never incarcerated was Jack's payments to clients and creditors, and how he made the law firm right enough with the world.[47]

*   *

---

[47] "From practicing law to changing it," by Dawn Turner Trice. Chicago Tribune August 1, 2010. http://articles.chicagotribune.com/2010-08-01/news/ct-met-trice-0802-20100801_1_law-license-law-firm-ex-offenders

II. **AND PROMISE**

A. **COFFIELD'S FEE**

I went to see a friend in his silk stocking law office after Jack threatened to summon the authorities if my family did not hand over half a million dollars. My friend looked at me and said:

"You need a white-collar criminal defense guy, and that's not me. You know that, right?"

Of course, right. And I knew whom to call: Mike Coffield. Mike was the Dean of Gentleman Lawyers in Chicago. He was the lawyer's lawyer of his time, and likely never to be matched in character, kindness, creativity and chutzpah. He was also a former opponent and close friend of mine who when he described his law practice said, "I only do trouble."

Before the U.S. Supreme Court, Mike opened an argument by telling the Court the point of law at issue was so important and warranted such legal clarity that he didn't care if his client won or lost; he cared only that the Court would deliver "The Big 9-0," one way or the other. That was Mike. And he got the 9-0 in that case – for his client.

I'd met Mike several years earlier when I'd sued one of his high profile clients over something potentially public and embarrassing. He called me within minutes of the time I faxed a demand letter to his client. Mike asked me to stay my hand until we could talk. "Your client's case is a good one. No B.S." He offered to bring donuts and coffee to my office on the following Saturday morning, and we would discuss the case.

When Mike saw my antiquarian book collection of nearly 3,000 volumes on custom shelving at my office, he totally disarmed me by engaging me for nearly two hours in a wide-ranging discussion about great literature and book collecting.

We discussed our case for about 5 minutes, after which Mike put a take-it-or-leave-it settlement number on the table that was a bit more than necessary to settle the case and far more than necessary for me to make a healthy contingent fee. He was well protecting his client. We settled the case on the spot because I had authority to settle for less (which I'm quite sure he correctly surmised).

Over the years, I had built enough good will and rapport with Mike and his staff so when I called him in distress, and his assistant answered the phone, she not only took me quite seriously when

I told her I was in trouble, but she insisted I wait by the phone while she contacted Mike.

Within five minutes Mike called me. He had excused himself from a meeting with clients far more important than I was, certainly.

"Mikee, what's wrong?," he asked with the gravelly, avuncular tone that could calm any storm. (Mike had always called me "Mikee." No one in my life except my grandmother had ever gotten away with that.)

"Trust account issues, Mike. And it's all going to come out," I said, on the verge of tears. I was so ashamed and embarrassed I had to call someone I admired so much personally and professionally, and whom I knew admired me.

"Mikee, go home and wait for me. I'll be there as soon as I can; in a few hours. Tell me your address."

I was stunned. Mike owed me nothing. I was speechless. But, as I would do repeatedly and often until Mike died in March 2007, I did what he told me to do.

In the early evening, Mike showed up at my home. He sat me down at my dining room table and listened long and hard. I told him everything.

When I was through, he reached across the table and took my hand.

"You're not going to jail. I won't let that happen. And anyway, most of the lawyers who hear this story will know it could have been them going from grey to dark. This whole thing is legal ethics twisting 'normal' ethics."

My immediate concern was jail, not Mike's reflection on ethics.

"Mike, you know you can't insure that. How can you say that?" I was relieved he ventured that far but was concerned he was unduly optimistic. We were talking about half a million dollars in trust account violations and a litany of other horribles.

"Mikee, no one I know professionally will believe I could possibly advise you to do what I'm about to suggest. But I know it'll keep you out of jail. I could be wrong, but I doubt it. I've never advised any client to do this, but I'm going to do it now. Ready?"

How could I not be ready? My heart pounded with my first salient self-hatred.

"Waive the attorney-client privilege and the Fifth Amendment, and testify if you must, without immunity."

"What? You're serious?"

"Totally serious. That's what Richard Secord did in Iran-Contra and he avoided prison. How much more accountable could you be than that? Think about it. It's the fastest way to get this behind you and your family. No matter what happens, you can always hold your head high and know you did the right thing. And most importantly, you can always hold yourself up as an example in the future when your kids make mistakes and you need to teach them accountability. Plus, you'll give me the most ammunition I could possibly have with the authorities. I'll always be able to say you did the right thing, and in mitigation when it comes to sentencing, I think that's what will get you probation and not jail."

Despite the fear and bad judgment that had made clear thinking so difficult for so long at that point in my life, something allowed me to hear Mike. I knew he was right.

"I'll do it."

"Don't you want to think about it? It's a huge step. Like I said, no one I know professionally will ever believe I advised you to do this."

"Let's do it."

I walked Mike to his car. I asked him what he meant about legal ethics twisting 'normal' ethics. He said little, but this:

"Well, we lawyers forget to think about harm when we think about how to solve problems. We can become divorced from right and wrong if we're not careful. Self-interest and greed really take over. We forget to protect our souls. I know that sounds really Catholic but I mean it. That's what happened to you, basically. You have a soul; you just forgot."

Within a day or two, through Mike, I voluntarily offered to turn in my law license. Shortly thereafter I offered the Cook County State's Attorney a one - count plea.

It took over a year for Mike to work out the details, but he did it. And from that night forward I began to approach my life with the seeds of a long-to-emerge clarity; seeds I now believe but for Mike might never have been planted. And I avoided prison.

At some point early in the process of winding up the law firm and working out matters with the Illinois Supreme Court and the State's Attorney, I asked Mike:

"Why are you helping me? You know by the time we clean this up I'll owe you so much money it will take years for me to pay you - if I ever can." Mike's answer:

"First of all, Mikee, we lawyers ought all operate on the 'there-but-for-the-grace-of-God-go-I' theory. You watch: of all the people you'll encounter from now on who know what you did and what happened, or what will happen to you, the least judgmental of them will be us lawyers. And don't forget, for the most part, the people who will handle and decide your matter and fate over this will be lawyers, too. I have faith in lawyers. That's part of why I don't think you'll go to jail."

"Secondly, I'm helping you because not so long ago, when I needed help in my own life, someone who owed me nothing reached out and helped me in a way that mattered, and was a turning point in my life. I asked him why he was helping me when he owed me nothing. He told me because at a crucial time in his life someone had reached out and helped him, and when he had asked why this man was helping him when he owed him nothing, he said someone who owed him nothing had reached out and helped him when he needed help badly."

"So, Mikee, that's just the way it goes. Here's my fee for helping you: from now on in your life there will be many people who show up on your doorstep with a backpack full of bricks, and they'll need you to remove those bricks one by one. And you'll be in a position to help them. So, help them. Lighten their load. That's how you're going to repay me."

*   *

B. **Voodoo Ethics**

"If you want to know the law and nothing else, you must look at it as a bad man, who cares only for material consequences which such knowledge enables him to predict, not as a good one, who finds his reasons for conduct, whether inside the law or outside of it, in the vaguer sanctions of conscience."

> Oliver Wendell Holmes, Jr.
> The Path of the Law, in
> COLLECTIVE LEGAL PAPERS
> 167, 171 (1920)

"You shall not . . . place a stumbling block before the blind."
> Leviticus 19:14

"... [L]et us stop passing judgment on one another. Instead, make up your mind not to put any stumbling block or obstacle in your brother's way."
> Romans 14:13

Neither God nor the Bible became my new best friend when I was in the throes of my 1997 turmoil. It was Mike Coffield who referred me to the passages I've quoted from Holmes, Leviticus and Romans.

I'd told Mike how crushed I was my extended family was retreating from me, and a beloved relative had snidely claimed there were no books to guide my family in how to deal with me. For them a felony conviction and possible prison term would shake the upper middle class order.

Mike made me reflect enough, even at my worst, to realize I had become a practitioner of voodoo ethics first, and of law, second. He said my family, sadly, was throwing obstacles at me in my blindness. He also said: "Maybe it runs in your family."

Mike gingerly observed how in my life and law practice, I too had been throwing obstacles before the blind and my brothers for too long, as a person and lawyer; doing things in the name of what was legal (sometimes), or simply what seemed expedient for me or my clients.

I'd like to think I've reversed that. I'd like to think I'm finally in a decent position to make sense of my voodoo ethics, to identify, minimally, where in the legal profession voodoo ethics are so insidious, and maybe offer a few inherently restorative solutions. I do think the way most lawyers are taught and apply legal ethics in the context of the adversarial system is, essentially, placing stumbling blocks before the (figuratively) blind and literally before our fellow human beings. It's voodoo ethics.

Voodoo ethics can go both ways. Lawyers and clients can be skilled practitioners. In what follows, I waver depending on the situation as to when the legal profession should protect clients first, and when I think the profession should protect its brothers and sisters from clients, and when I think the profession should protect lawyers from themselves and each other. It's a mixed bag.

Too many lawyers would scoff at an "ethical' rule that presses a practicing lawyer to make decisions using a conventional, non-legal ethical definition, rather than the pure self-interest which the adversarial system promotes so coldly and boldly.

In real life, i.e., outside of the legal profession, "ethics" is supposedly a core principle of good, and concerns itself with the values, obligations, rights and duties of individuals, communities or institutions vis à vis each other. The fundamental principle of any code of ethics except, it seems, in the legal profession, is that no action is "ethical" if it ignores the inviolate character of human nature and the supposed sanctity of human dignity. We don't put stumbling blocks before the blind, presumably.

But the "ethics" of the legal profession routinely allow lawyers to ignore much of this when expedient, while too many of its wise men argue that advancing the sacrosanct client's best interest is the "good" that defines the profession's real code of "ethics." This rub results in voodoo ethics.

Voodoo ethics is basically the convergence of opportunity, self-interest, greed and the brains or power to manipulate rules legally regardless of what harm results.

Self-interest and greed grow in proportion as they are fed.[48] They were the main forces driving most of my clients. And I lost sight of how low and ugly many of them were, because I was busy applying voodoo ethics to represent them in the adversary system. I hadn't really considered any of this before Mike Coffield opened my eyes.

---

[48] I first discovered the notion of "greed growing in proportion as it is fed" after my disbarment when I read "The Cost of Something for Nothing," a small tract by a former Illinois Governor (no irony intended). See Altgeld, John Peter. 1904. The Cost of Something for Nothing. Chicago: The Hammersmark Pub. Co. Perhaps the leading scholar on lawyer dishonesty and the culture of greed in the legal profession is Professor Lisa Lerman, whose work includes studies of client trust account problems and the more prevalent but less detected form of theft from clients: billing and expense fraud. See, e.g., Ethical Problems in The Practice of Law. 2nd ed. New York: Aspen, 2008 (with Philip Schrag); "Greed among

The queen of my voodoo ethics clients was an art wholesaler who got in hot water with a Las Vegas casino. Her story and her conduct aren't so different from the stories and conduct of which I was routinely the steward for many of my clients. The casino discovered how for years she had been misusing the sizeable credit lines they'd extended to her: $40,000-$50,000 of chips per junket.

Rather than gamble with the chips, she had a revolving stable of gigolos slowly cash in most of the chips over a matter of days, while she sat at the tables gambling precious little - for show. She also paid the young men with borrowed chips, and then used the remaining cash to buy art, consigned the art to retail art dealers, and as the retailers would pay her she would periodically and slowly repay the casino.

This worked for a while, but when art sales slowed and she repaid way too slowly, she could no longer keep the casino from looking the other way, or from just not looking. I asked if it ever occurred to her that interest-free inventory financing might not have been what the casino intended.

American Lawyers." Oklahoma City University Law Review 31 (2006): 611. "Billing Fraud versus Misappropriation: A Double Standard for Lawyer Dishonesty." Hofstra Law Review 34 (2006): 847.

She laughed and said: "Baby, business is anything you can get away with short of a felony conviction."

This was surely the mentality also displayed by my biggest client and its General Counsel, when through him the client set out to and did legally cheat our firm out of money, and made bogus billing fraud claims while they postured.

In felony's mirror, I see the art dealer and General Counsel reflected in my conduct as a person and lawyer.

In "The Purposes of Legal Ethics and the Primacy of Practice," Professor Robert Burns observed that "[e]thical lawyering requires not only knowledge of rules, but also ethical dispositions and virtues."[49]

I lacked ethical dispositions and virtues when I needed them most, i.e., when I was staring in the face of an enemy client whose only virtue was the bottom line.

I confronted my enemy. I called this new General Counsel's billing fraud claims and his refusal to pay our 20% fee "trumped up." He laughed.

---

[49] Robert P. Burns, The Purposes of Legal Ethics and the Primacy of Practice, 39 Wm. & Mary L. Rev. 327(1998), , citing Andreas Eshete, Does a Lawyer's Character Matter?, in THE GOOD LAWYER: LAWYERS' ROLES AND LAWYERS' ETHICS 259-69 (David Luban ed., 1984) (discussing the complexities inherent in professional morality), at 270-85 (discussing the effects of a lawyer's personal conduct on his character); Gerald J. Postema, Self-Image, Integrity, and Professional Responsibility, in THE GOOD LAWYER, id., at 286-314 (discussing the moral psychology aspect of the lawyers role); Williams, Id.,, at 259-69 (discussing the importance of "professional dispositions").http://scholarship.law.wm.edu/wmlr/vol3 9/iss2/3

As if honoring a contract would be unethical since paying per its terms would not be in the client's "best interest," the General Counsel coolly claimed it was his duty to the shareholders of his publicly held client, and their bottom line, to assert these claims "without regard for their transparent appearance." This was voodoo ethics; the ethics of harm with a new name.

In his essay, "The Adversary System Excuse," Professor David Luban has described precisely what my client's General Counsel articulated in less delicate terms: the fallacy of a lawyer's "Principle of Moral Nonaccountability" according to which, "[i]f advocates restrain their zeal because of moral compunctions, they are not fulfilling their assigned role in the adversary proceeding,..."[50]

---

[50] THE GOOD LAWYER: LAWYERS' ROLES AND LAWYERS' ETHICS 90 (D. Luban ed. 1983). *See also*, Professor Monroe Friedman's seminal work, Lawyers' Ethics in the Adversary System. Freedman, Monroe H. 1975. Lawyers' ethics in an adversary system. Indianapolis: Bobbs-Merrill.

I no longer buy "the Adversary System Excuse," but I lived, breathed and believed it until my own client used it against us, and I felt like the bad guy in the end of a B western who can't believe he got shot. I learned then that voodoo ethics don't know honor, boundaries or loyalty.

Like the old senior partner told me in the bathroom so early in my career: "there's nothing your biggest client can't do for you or to you."

Depending upon one's moral center or relative sense of ethics, some might say it was smart, wrong, or incumbent upon my client's General Counsel to assert his "excessive" fee defense – for its strategic and tactical value, and without regard for the ethics of this meritless position. Or, did his legal position derive its "merit" because it was so strategic and tactical? I'd like to think most lawyers would say "absolutely not." Certainly, that is what most people would say.

Regardless, my experience illustrates in so many ways not just voodoo ethics in law, but also the basis for examining key issues law students, lawyers and business people grapple with constantly, always have grappled with, and always will. The adversarial system is one culprit. But it's our system and mostly, it's human nature. It's devised specifically not only to allow but also to encourage the putting of stumbling blocks before our brothers and the blind.

So that said, to sensitize the reader to voodoo ethics, and maybe provoke thought and some promise for improvement, I make some comments derived from my experience with the dark sides of black letter law.[51]

*   *

---

[51] Generally accepted and rarely doubted legal principles.

I. **Fiduciary Duties**

The lawyer's roles of fiduciary and agent in
relation to the client limit his or her autonomy.
A fiduciary is "a person holding the character of a
trustee, ... to act primarily for the benefit of
another in matters connected with his
undertaking."[52] A lawyer has a fiduciary
relationship with his client.[53] An agent is "a
person authorized by another to act for him, one
entrusted with another's business.[54]

A lawyer often serves as the agent of his client.
Common examples: when, on behalf of a client, a
lawyer makes a contract offer, or pays money by
the client, the lawyer is acting as the client's
agent.

A more problematic example of fiduciary and
agent: the lawyer holds money in trust "on behalf"
of a client who is openly keeping rightly owed
money from a creditor, while the client is lying
about it to shareholders, the SEC and possibly a
bankruptcy court, and the lawyer knows this.

---

[52] BLACK'S LAW DICTIONARY 752 (4th ed. 1951)(if the
reader wonders why such an old edition: it was my
Dad's).

[53] *Id.*, at 753.

[54] *Id.*, at 85.

A well-known rule or law of lawyers that arises
from the fiduciary ethics that traditionally
characterize the attorney-client relationship is
one about which laypersons are generally familiar:
a lawyer is obligated to represent a client with
zeal and diligence within the bounds of the law.[55]

That's the easy part, because in studying this rule
as a law or business student, or when cases have
been litigated in this arena, the focus tends to be
on what happens when the lawyer's *lack* of zeal
becomes neglect.[56]

It's less common for the zeal inquiry to focus on
what happens when a lawyer is *too* zealous, and his
or her zeal encroaches on ethical and moral
boundaries, as I feel occurred in my case. My
comments here thus focus on the extent and
limits of zeal-driven fiduciary obligations.

---

[55] In re Ring, 565 N.E.2d 983 (Ill. 1990).

[56] Neglect of a client's affairs is misconduct that can
warrant disciplinary sanctions, In re Levine, 463
N.E.2d 715 (Ill. 1984), which can be appropriate even
when the lawyer lacks a corrupt motive or moral
turpitude. *Id.* In Colorado, Colo.RPC 1.3 requires an
attorney to act with reasonable diligence in
representing a client and prohibits an attorney from
neglecting a client's legal matter.

Philosopher Elliot L. Cohen has with some notoriety questioned the morality of lawyers, and argued that the "adversary ethic" is unsound, that critics of the "adversary ethic" believe it "is a claim of moral immunity for lawyers, and an excuse for lawyer immorality."[57]

Professor David Luban, quotes Andreas Eshete, saying that "[e]ffective adversarial advocacy ... demands measures that are unacceptable from a moral point of view ... A firm and settled disposition to truthfulness, fairness, goodwill, and the like would thwart the lawyer's capacity to do his tasks well. To excel as a lawyer, it would be beneficial to possess combative character traits such as cunning."[58]

---

[57] Cohen, Pure Legal Advocates and Moral Agents: Two Concepts of a Lawyer in an Adversary System, 4 CRIM. JUST. ETHICS 38 (Winter/Spring, 1985).

[58] LAWYERS AND JUSTICE 109 (1988).

While not directly a proponent, Professor Luban himself described a lawyer's "Principle of Moral Nonaccountability" according to which, "[i]f advocates restrain their zeal because of moral compunctions, they are not fulfilling their assigned role in the adversary proceeding."[59]

Richard Wasserstrom says "[c]onventional wisdom has it that . . . where the attorney-client relationship exists, it is often appropriate and many times even obligatory for the attorney to do things that, all other things being equal, an ordinary person need not, and should not do. What is characteristic of this role of a lawyer is the lawyer's required indifference to a wide variety of ends and consequences that in other contexts would be of undeniable moral significance."[60]

---

[59] The Adversary System Excuse, in THE GOOD LAWYER: LAWYERS' ROLES AND LAWYERS' ETHICS 90 (D. Luban ed. 1983)(collection of essays that examine lawyer's professional roles and personal morality).

[60] Lawyers as Professionals: Some Moral Issues, in ETHICS AND THE LEGAL PROFESSION 117 (M. Davis & F. Elliston ed. 1986)

Today, as a disbarred felon reflecting on my law practice and legal transgressions, I read Wasserstrom's comments and wonder when as a lawyer I ceased to be an "ordinary person" who willingly embraced "indifference to a wide variety of ends and consequences that in other contexts would be of undeniable moral significance."

I wonder if I can become once again "ordinary." Or did law school change me and every other lawyer irretrievably from being "ordinary" into something else?

When did such voodoo ethics become acceptable? And, why? Representing clients with my art dealer's mentality didn't help, nor did having enemies like my client's General Counsel.

In my case, our client didn't break the law. Rather, through its General Counsel, the client took positions that voodoo ethics and the law of the adversary system allowed: harsh, fabricated positions asserted for strategic and tactical value, with complete and intentional disregard for whether these positions had any legal merit or factual basis, and without regard for what harm such positions would cause.

*   *

2. **Attorney-Client Fee Agreements**

A client may always discharge a lawyer at any
time, with or without cause. A lawyer who is
discharged without cause is not entitled to
recover contract fees from the client, but is
entitled to fees calculated only on a *quantum
meruit* basis (the reasonable value of services
rendered) for the services rendered before the
client fired the lawyer.[61]

Scenario: By simply terminating the lawyer
(without cause) and thereby putting into play the
question of reasonable value of services rendered,
a business executive or a general counsel can
create the opportunity probably to save a lot of
money, or minimally to lever a negotiation of
legal fees the company has already agreed to pay
for services already rendered by the lawyer.

Most courts nationwide do or would strongly
disagree with me. But freedom of contract, not
courts and juries, ultimately should govern

---

[61] The applicable Illinois and Colorado law is basically
the same on this point. Balla v. Gambro, 584 N.E.2d
104 (Ill. 1991); Rhoades v. Norfolk & W. Ry., 399
N.E.2d 969, 974 (Ill. 1979); Jenkins v. District Court,
676 P.2d 1201, 1204 (Colo. 1984); Olsen and Brown v.
City of Englewood, 889 P.2d 673, 675 (Colo. 1995).

resolution of disputes relating to fee agreements between lawyers and clients. Otherwise, the law provides endless opportunities for abuse born from voodoo ethics.

On the one hand, as the law is now, any client can essentially disavow a fee agreement and its terms simply by claiming, usually with the "advice" (or meddling) from another attorney, the fee was "excessive" and a court or jury should be the final arbiter. The social cost in this scenario, and drain on the public in engaging the court system, is too high because the free hand of the market isn't in control.

If freedom of contract ruled, the temptation for voodoo ethics and abuses of the adversarial system would be controlled by the free hand of the market. Clients and lawyers would know a deal is a deal. Each side would always be free to engage counsel of their own to represent and negotiate their interests at the time they make their deal, i.e., when they consummate an attorney-client relationship with a fee agreement.

The potential for harmful absurdity and abuse is less if freedom of contract prevails rather than courts and juries. A client is likely only going to hire only one lawyer to negotiate on their behalf for purposes of engaging another lawyer. It's not normal for that same client to engage yet another lawyer to engage a lawyer to engage a lawyer. Rationality is more likely this way. But without the rule of freedom of contract, voodoo ethics and the potential abuses of the adversary system lurk around every corner every time a large amount of money changes hands or a large and rightly earned legal fee becomes due.

*   *

3. Attorneys' Fees: Excessive or Reasonable?

Courts are duty-bound to guard against the collection of excessive legal fees, both contingent and fixed.[62] Where there is an unconscionable fee alleged to exist, the matter is subject to action by the disciplinary regulators.[63] While a contingent fee contract may be valid when it is formed, if a subsequent dispute arises, the court can still ensure the fee is not excessive,[64] and will consider evidence of reasonableness even if the

---

[62] Illinois cases: XL Disposal Corp. v. John Sexton Contractors Co., 659 N.E.2d 1312, 1315 (Ill. 1995); In re Teichner, 470 N.E.2d 972 (Ill. 1984); Gasperini v. Gasperini, 373 N.E.2d 576 (Ill. App. 1st Dist. 1978) ($20,000 fee in divorce proceeding that involved a $24,000 property settlement was excessive). Colorado cases: A lawyer is entitled to be paid a reasonable fee for the services that he is requested to provide. The reasonableness of attorney's fees are subject to scrutiny by courts pursuant to their supervisory powers. Law Offices of J.E. Losavio, Jr. v. Law Firm of Michael W. McDivitt, P.C., 865 P.2d 934, 935 (Colo. App. 1993); People v. Nutt, 696 P.2d 242, 248 (Colo. 1984). Colo.RPC 1.5 defines factors relevant to determination of reasonableness, which factors the courts follow. E.g., Tallitsch v. Child Support Services, Inc., 926 P.2d 143 (Colo. App. 1996), cert. denied, Nov. 12, 1996.

[63] In re Kutner, 399 N.E.2d 963, 965 (Ill. 1979) (lawyer censured where he received an excessive fee for representing client in criminal battery case).

[64] In re Doyle, 581 N.E.2d 669, 674 (Ill. 1991).

parties entered into an express contract for the disputed fee.[65]

In Maksym v. Loesch, 937 F.2d 1237 (7th Cir. 1991), a lawyer sued his client to recover on a contract for attorneys' fees. One of the client's defenses: the fee was excessive and violated Rule 2-106 of the Illinois Rules of Professional Responsibility. The Court of Appeals for the Seventh Circuit, applying Illinois law, found that a contract for professional services can be unenforceable if contrary to public policy. The court stated that not every violation of professional ethics rules makes a lawyer's contract with the client voidable per se, but "conduct which violates both professional ethics and contract law, such as the charging of exorbitant fees, is not placed beyond the reach of contract law because it violates professional standards as well." Maksym, 937 F.2d at 1244.

---

[65] McCracken & McCracken, P.C. v. Haegele, 618 N.E.2d 577, 581-82 (Ill. App. 4th Dist. 1993). In re Doyle, 581 N.E.2d 669, 674 (Ill. 1991), In re Teichner, 470 N.E.2d 972 (Ill. 1984); In re Marriage of Pagano, 607 N.E.2d 1242, 1249-50 (Ill. 1993).

Imagine if a borrower could call the bank and say "Hey, my interest rate is excessive. I'm not paying that. I want a jury to decide it." A bank has no less power over a borrower than an attorney has over a client when negotiating a fee and terms of an attorney-client relationship. But we all know consumers of bank services have no similar "protections."

Similarly, doctors and hospitals are in no less of a fiduciary relation to patients than lawyers are to clients. Yet we tolerate medical debts as the biggest cause for personal bankruptcy in America. Perhaps medical patients should have summary judgment proof excessive fee defenses to medical billing the way clients have such defenses against lawyers. I say that facetiously. The courts are already sufficiently crowded.

Bankers and doctors can argue that loan borrowers or medical patients differ from clients of lawyers, but do they? All three are each free to go elsewhere if they don't like the terms. Or, are none that free?

Similarly, loan borrowers and medical patients are no less vulnerable when they enter into contracts, nor more easily able to understand loan terms or medical services agreements than they are able to understand payment and other terms in an attorney-client fee agreement. Yet not even the financial and medical industry disciplinary regulators presume to know more about contracting than the parties to the contract.

Consumers of legal services should be no different. If clients with voodoo ethics wish to undo a fee agreement, they should be held to the rules of the game for all other contracts.

*   *

4. Clients: Sophisticated or Unsophisticated?

My bias is obviously against clients who are prejudicially far more sophisticated than the lawyers and law firms who represent them.[66]

Further, courts that regulate disputes that can turn on the client's relative sophistication are in no better a position to resolve these disputes than the parties to the contracts who come before the courts. Plenty of judges and bar disciplinary counsel would argue otherwise.

My proposed solution: a client's sophistication should be one of the codified factors in state supreme court rules applied in attorney-client disputes to determine when attorneys' fees are reasonable or not excessive.

---

[66] *See, e.g.,* Cohen v. Radio-Electronics Officers Union, 679 A.2d 1188 (N.J. 1996). The New Jersey Supreme Court held unenforceable a provision negotiated by sophisticated parties in which the client was required to give the lawyer six months' notice before it could terminate the contract. The Court held that this provision chilled the client's right to terminate its relationship with the lawyer. *Id.,* at 1197 - 1201. The Court supplanted the parties' judgment and intent with its own when it concluded, however, that the lawyer was entitled to "reasonable" notice of termination, which it determined was one month rather than the three days the client gave.

A prime example of the dangerous sophisticated client is the client like my former client, or even a less sophisticated client who is nevertheless sufficiently sophisticated to use the time value of money as a weapon against the lawyer, wreak havoc on the lawyer and to consume substantial judicial resources in the name of saving a buck while applying voodoo ethics.

The case of McKenzie Construction, Inc. v. V.L. Maynard, is a prime example[67] of precisely the type of Dickensian litigation path we feared in our dispute with our client; a dispute where it's plain a chiseling client has taken advantage of legal rules governing courts' supervision of attorneys' fees, and where even the court itself can't agree on applicable principles or the reasons for the outcome of the dispute.

Plaintiff, McKenzie Construction, Inc., appealed from a district court judgment refusing to set aside as "not clearly excessive" a contingent attorney fee agreement with the defendant, attorney Desmond L. Maynard.

---

[67] McKenzie Construction, Inc. v. V.L. Maynard, 758 F.2d 97 (3rd Cir. 1985).

It was undisputed the plaintiff had expressly told the lawyer he did not have enough money to pay the lawyer's quoted hourly rate, so the parties agreed on a one-third contingent fee.

When the lawyer *too* expeditiously achieved the client's desired result by settlement, the client objected to the fee on the rank hindsight theory that had the lawyer been retained to charge hourly, the resulting fee would have been less than one tenth of the one-third contingent fee.[68]

Were the dispute in McKenzie an ordinary commercial contract, there is no way any court would have entertained this client's argument absent clear and convincing evidence of fraud, overreaching or undue influence. But this is a sacrosanct attorney-client fee dispute, regardless of how trumped up the client's claim.

---

[68] I had many clients - including a family member for whom I recovered $1 million - make this fallacious assertion to me over the years, and it routinely made my blood boil. Two very sophisticated clients of Jack's also made this very argument, and together we litigated that case for five years through the trial and appellate process, and then even when one of these clients filed for bankruptcy. Their clear intent was plainly to stiff Jack or chisel him into submission.

So, the dispute required both a federal district court and appeals court to devote substantial resources to reach a non-unanimous and rather contentious result – over less than $100,000.

The U.S. District Court upheld the contingent fee as not "clearly excessive." So the client appealed, claiming the district court abused its discretion as to its application of the correct legal standards, i.e., if the fee was not "clearly excessive," as distinct from the lesser standard which the client urged the court to adopt: simply "unreasonable."

Siding with the client, the Court of Appeals for the Third Circuit explained the difference and why it mattered - at least to that court. " 'Clearly excessive' ... is the standard for an ethical violation under Disciplinary Rule 2-106(A) of the ABA Model Code of Professional Responsibility. However, we are convinced that in a civil action, a fee may be found to be 'unreasonable' and therefore subject to appropriate reduction by a court without necessarily being so 'clearly excessive' to justify a finding of a breach of ethics."

Worse yet, in my view, the client also appealed on the basis that the district court erred by limiting his consideration to "circumstances which existed at the time the agreement was entered into." [citations omitted].

Of course, this is the only basis any court will ever construe or interpret any other ordinary contract. Indeed, this was exactly the Third Circuit's observation, except this observation was made as partial support for *vacating* the district court's decision and remanding the matter for hearing, despite finding the plaintiff client a sophisticated businessman.

The Third Circuit stated in vacating the district court:

> "We believe that the district court had too narrow a view. Because courts have a special concern to supervise contingent attorney fee agreements, they are not to be enforced on the same basis as ordinary commercial contracts.... [citations omitted]
>
> We, therefore, conclude that the rule announced by the district court contained legal error to the extent that it excluded relevant factors other than those existing at the time the fee agreement was executed."

From a legal or academic perspective, a further frustrating aspect of this decision is how the potentially concurring opinion reads like a potentially notable dissent. But as a concurrence it offers empty while pointedly apt criticism of the majority opinion. As a concurrence, the stated problems with the majority opinion reduce to rubbish plain common sense and what absolutely should be the law pertaining to undisputedly sophisticated clients:

> [T]his case involves an arm's-length agreement between a sophisticated businessperson and an attorney who offered to undertake the representation at issue on a non-contingent basis.

> ...[B]y focusing the inquiry upon the circumstances existing after a successful result has been achieved, the court will invite litigation over most contingent fee arrangements...

> ...[M]ost American jurisdictions recognize that competent persons are free to contract for legal services on terms that are mutually satisfactory to the client and the lawyer, including terms in which the attorney's compensation depends upon a successful outcome.

> ...[A] degree of scrutiny which subjected every fee contract to an after-the-event examination by the court would, I fear, limit the undoubted utility of contingent fee arrangements, by substituting a court-

determined fee for that which was bargained for by the parties.

In its hortatory and lofty doctrine as to the ostensible sanctity and extent of a lawyer's fiduciary duty to the clients, I feel this Third Circuit decision strikes at the heart of what's wrong with this aspect of the law of lawyers, because in real life this sort of thinking can severely prejudice lawyers and large or small firms when their clients have voodoo ethics.

It's treacherous when the important or long-time corporate client is sufficiently sophisticated that if it chooses to do so, it can tie its lawyer or law firm and the judiciary up in knots; it can complain about client service, manner of delivery, pricing, reasonableness of fees for services rendered, assessment of services rendered, and the like.

This problem can be compounded by the existence of consultants (some of whom are former lawyers) who with possibly benign intent advise on the management of attorney-client relationships.

An over-zealous in-house lawyer can wreak havoc on a company's outside counsel when armed with a consultant's unwitting roadmap for throwing all kinds of potentially harmful obstacles at a law firm.[69]

To me, the Third Circuit's circuitous reasoning is the type that provides valid arguments for a client's relative sophistication to matter. When a client is sophisticated, that should be a *dispositive factor* when courts resolve attorney client disputes. A sophisticated client should be held to his or her contract.

Courts won't say this. They are too careful and hate reversal. The regulators of the profession in each of the fifty states could say precisely this by promulgating such rules for application in fee disputes.

*   *

---

[69] *See, e.g.*, Patrick J. McKenna and Ronald F. Pol, Genuine Client Focus: Managing The Sophisticated Client's Expectations.
www.Mng_Sophisticated_Clients.pdf

5. Client Trust Accounts

"[W]e know that a small number of American lawyers are stealing at least $26 million per year, but that large figure probably represents only a fraction of the actual problem."

> Professor Lisa Lerman, in
> The Slippery Slope from Ambition
> to Greed to Dishonesty: Lawyers,
> Money and Professional Integrity
> (2002) [70]

Each of the 50 state supreme courts disbars handfuls of attorneys annually for invading client trust accounts.[71]

---

[70] Lerman, Lisa. The Slippery Slope from Ambition to Greed to Dishonesty: Lawyers, Money and Professional Integrity, 30 HOFSTRA L. REV. 879 (2002).

[71] For a discussion of various types of retainers and more details and rules of client trust accounting, see generally Di Pippa, John, Lawyers, Clients, and Money, 18 UALR L. J. 95 (1995-1996)(Arkansas is the model to an extent but general principles apply). Most if not all of the fifty state supreme courts publish extensive trust accounting manuals for lawyers.

These hundreds of lawyers who are disbarred annually, nationwide, for invading trust accounts, are *those who got caught*.[72]

Nationwide the profession disbars literally hundreds of lawyers annually, because lawyers are allowed to sign on these accounts and are usually guilty of "knowing misappropriation" (a walk-and-talk-like-a-duck concept: the lawyer knows the client hasn't authorized the lawyer to use the client's funds held in the trust account).[73]

---

[72] As of 2010, in the 29 years of New Jersey's Random Audit Program (RAP) for client trust accounts, 73 lawyers were caught and disbarred, and 16 suspended. These disbarred (73) and suspended (16) attorneys accounted for 59% of all the attorneys disciplined as a result of New Jersey's RAP program. 2010 State of the Attorney Disciplinary System Report, at 24. ("New Jersey Disciplinary System Report") http://www.judiciary.state.nj.us/oae/AttorneyDisciplin aryReport.pdf.

[73] Client trust account violations may be the largest single cause for lawyer *disbarment* (except maybe in some states, in some years, client neglect), but billing and expense fraud by lawyers is thought to be where far more and most of the stealing from clients occurs; but it's harder to detect than client fund misappropriation. Lerman, Lisa. A Double Standard for Lawyer Dishonesty: Billing Fraud versus Misappropriation, 34 HOFSTRA L. REV. 847 (2006).

The quantum of dollars held annually and in fact mishandled in client trust funds is probably incalculable.

For example, on average, in New Jersey alone, clients entrust New Jersey lawyers with almost $3 billion dollars in primary client trust accounts, and even more in separate fiduciary accounts relating to estates, guardianships, receiverships, trusteeships and other fiduciary capacities.[74]

Only a few states have random audit programs,[75] which means the majority of lawyers who get caught are caught because something goes wrong and they are affirmatively reported.

There is a solution: Take trust account signing privileges away from lawyers, and no one needs to worry how big this problem really is, since this problem will evaporate, and lawyers can no longer harm clients or the profession in this way.

---

[74] New Jersey Disciplinary System Report, *Id.*, n. 72 at 59.

[75] New Jersey has the largest lawyer population in the country subject to a random auditing program. "Only eight (8) other states have operational random programs. In order of implementation, they are: Iowa (1973), Delaware (1974), washington (1977), New Hampshire, (1980), North Carolina (1984), Vermont (1990), Kansas (2000) and Connecticut (2007)." *Id.*

In my biased view, my story alone should be
proof enough why lawyers should not sign on
client trust accounts. I'm one of thousands of
lawyers who have been disbarred for exactly the
same thing. And there are many thousands more
who do or have done the same thing but have not
been caught.

I don't argue that lawyers should not use trust
accounts. That's fine. But let a bank or title
company fill the role of professional escrow
agent. There is no practical or policy reason for
lawyers to be the signatories. We are just too
human to resist this temptation, and we are
terrible bookkeepers.

The state supreme courts and their disciplinary
regulators run the judiciary branches of state
government. They are the lawmakers and law
enforcers of lawyers. And they don't hesitate to
sanction individual lawyers who violate fiduciary
standards. But in my view, the profession's
guardians don't act like fiduciaries for the public
given the profession's perpetual failure to solve
invasion or mishandling of client trust accounts,
when the solution is so obvious.

Voodoo ethics are powerful. Bar scions might say, accurately, that all 50 states have their own versions of detailed regulations, monitoring systems, proscriptions and admonitions governing lawyers who handle client funds, and in every state a portion of every lawyer's bar dues pays for an overdraft monitoring and client security trust fund intended to compensate clients who are victims of lawyer theft.[76]

What bar scions don't regulate and what lawyers are not required to tell clients before accepting their money for deposit into lawyer-controlled trust accounts, is every client security trust fund in the United States limits the amount a client can recover. If a client's loss exceeds the maximum allowed for any one client, the only recourse is to sue the lawyer.

---

[76] Overdraft detection programs require financial institutions report to the bar regulators whenever a lawyer's trust account check is presented against insufficient funds. In the 25 years of New Jersey's overdraft detection program, it "has been the sole reason for the discipline of 144 New Jersey lawyers. Over half of the attorneys (53%) so disciplined were disbarred." This statistic is no bragging point and speaks volumes about the propensity of lawyers to overdraw trust accounts. So why let them operate such accounts? New Jersey Disciplinary System Report, *Id.*, n. 72 at 24.

The legal profession's apparent refusal to solve likely its biggest cause for disbarment arguably suggests the profession is truly committed to putting its own interests ahead of the public it claims to protect, rather than the reverse, as the notion of fiduciaries might suggest. [77]

This is a gross example of how the legal profession seems continually to blame the individual lawbreaking lawyers and figuratively speaking, also seems continually to scratch its head as to why the problem persists.

You can't get hit by a train unless standing on the tracks. Simply take clients off the tracks. No more harm. And no more bureaucratic machinery engaged by bar regulatory and disciplinary institutions to solve such a solvable problem. Otherwise, this entire matter remains a case of voodoo ethics.

---

[77] For an authoritative discussion of the profession's general advancement of its own self-interest ahead of the public interest, see Professor Deborah Rhode's In the Interests of Justice: Reforming the Legal Profession (New York: Oxford University Press, 2001)

One of the most obscene, obvious displays of why lawyers should not sign on trust accounts is the Louis Robles matter (circa 2007). Robles stole $13.5 million from his asbestos clients, who ultimately filed a class action claim for compensation against the Florid State Bar client security fund. The clients' claims were dismissed with prejudice.

Regardless of whether the legal reasoning was "sound," after several Miami federal judges recused themselves, U.S. District Judge Willis B. Hunt Jr. of Georgia ruled that the 11th Amendment of the US Constitution immunizes the Florida State Bar from the victim-clients' class action claim against the Bar's client security fund, because the fund is a regulatory arm of the state Supreme Court.[78]

To put it bluntly, a federal court ruled that the Florida State Bar was immune from trust account damage claims brought by victims the Bar supposedly protects. That to me is voodoo ethics, too.

---

[78] Compensation - Empty Handed, by Jordana Mishory, Daily Business Review, January 4, 2007 http://www.judicialaccountability.org/articles/lawyerke ptmoneyofasbestos.htm

Other representative incidents are no less egregious even when they involve far less money than the $13 million in the Robles mess.

Daniel Antonio Benito, of Miami, Florida, was permanently disbarred in August 2011.[79] Like a Ponzi scheme, Benito had established a three-year pattern of using client funds to satisfy past obligations to different clients. One of his clients claimed to have sent him $80,000 to fund a marital settlement agreement, which never materialized. Instead of depositing the money into his trust account until the conflict was resolved, Benito disbursed the funds to himself. The client demanded a refund through a new attorney, and that led to a fee dispute in addition to the claim for a refund of the money.[80] Repeated use of trust accounts by the lawyer who ultimately gets caught is very common. Bar regulators can't possibly think when a violation emerges, it's an isolated incident.

---

[79] Florida Supreme Court disciplines 22 attorneys (Case No. SC09-775).
http://www.jaxdailyrecord.com/showstory.php?Story_id=534159

[80] This is nearly the same factual scenario that arose in In re Himmel, *supra* n. 45, the Illinois Supreme Court case that first suspended an attorney for one year failing to report wrongdoing of another attorney.

In July, 2011, a horridly dark, ironic
demonstration of why lawyers should not sign
trust accounts emerged from California. A
former Santa Barbara lawyer who advertised
"Don't Let Others Steal Your Elderly Parent's
Estate" was disbarred after $367,409 went
missing from her client's estate.[81]   The
California Bar disbarred lawyer Sandra Jean
Smith when she couldn't produce the money
and then bounced a repayment check.

My views about trust accounts are no
indictment of lawyers. My views are an
argument *for* lawyers that acknowledges our
humanity and our weaknesses. Most lawyers do
not invade trust accounts. But this problem,
the profession's ability to solve it, and refusal
not to do so is voodoo ethics.

The refusal by leaders of the profession not to
implement a wholesale and simple solution
violates basic ethical notions. The essentially
utilitarian solution of taking trust account
signing powers away from lawyers is epitomized
by the essence of "Blackstone's ratio," i.e., his
classic statement that it's better for 10 guilty

---

[81] Lawyer Disbarred: Money Missing
   http://www.independent.com/news/2011/jul/05/lawyer-
disbarred/

people to go free rather than convict one innocent man.[82]

By the same token, it's incumbent on legal profession leaders to protect lawyers from themselves, because by protecting the bulk of lawyers from themselves who would never violate a trust account and need no protection, the profession can protect every client from any lawyer who may succumb to this entropy.

It seems the profession wrestles with this issue but doesn't want to go "all the way" with a clear solution, although one high court has come close but in a supremely twisted manner.

---

[82] 4 William Blackstone, Commentaries.

The Minnesota Supreme Court recently banned a lawyer for life from ever again signing on a client trust account after she made $144,000 of improper transfers from her firm's client trust account - arguing she used it only as a bank, to cover operating account overdrafts – to weather the stormy recession and lost client revenue. Instead of disbarment, the Minnesota Supreme Court suspended this lawyer for 18 months followed by three years probation.[83]

No harm no foul for stealing in Minnesota. This result and rationale is really voodoo ethics, because the court found "substantial mitigating circumstances" that saved this lawyer from disbarment, while finding this lawyer's clients had not been at risk because the money was repaid. That's like arguing check kiting doesn't put a bank at risk if the checks are ultimately covered.

---

[83] In re Petition for Disciplinary Action against Jo M. Fairbairn, a Minnesota Attorney, Registration No. 28137 (September 14, 2011). http://www.mncourts.gov/opinions/sc/current/OPA10 0977-0914.pdf

Before this result in Minnesota, it's been generally inconceivable any lawyer could get anything but disbarment for such a knowing misappropriation. Frankly, while the lifetime ban from being a trust account signatory makes sense, the rationale for the decision makes no sense and suggests that the Rule of Law when it comes to trust account defalcations is no rule at all.

For those in the bar who would argue client trust account violations are isolated to small firms or sole practitioners, where such problems are most common and where bar disciplinary counsel focus and predominate, large firms are not immune.[84]

---

[84] Small firm lawyers and solo practitioners are disciplined more often than those at large firms, but it's a mistake to think the conduct is isolated. *See, e,g.,* Lerman, Lisa. A Double Standard for Lawyer Dishonesty: Billing Fraud versus Misappropriation, 34 HOFSTRA L. REV. 847 (2006)., at n. 3., citing Leslie C. Levin, The Ethical World of Solo and Small Law Firm Practitioners, 41 HOUS. L. REV. 309, 310 (2004).

On September 21, 2011, news of a near $2.5 million client trust account theft was reported to have occurred in the New York City office of international law firm Crowell & Mooring.[85]

In most civilized cultures it has become talismanic that unless every person's rights are protected, the rights of no one are protected; protection of individual rights is the only way to protect a society.

The society of lawyers depends on the society of non-lawyers not just for its existence, but also for its credibility. We can't have a society of protectors that protects itself first. Too often, this is how non-lawyers view the legal profession, and that perception has everything to do with voodoo ethics.

*   *

---

[85] Crowell lawyer suspected of stealing $2.5 million arrested in Asia.
http://newsandinsight.thomsonreuters.com/Legal/Ne
ws/2011/09_-
_September/Crowell_lawyer_suspected_of_stealing_$2
_5_mln_arrested_in_Asia/

C.   **RESTORATIVE   JUSTICE   FOR
         WHITE-COLLAR CRIME**

> Zacchaeus...was also a master in white-collar theft. Tax collectors were outcasts in society - not just because they were collecting money for the Roman Empire, but because they appear to have been lining their own pockets at the same time. And as a chief tax collector we can assume that Zacchaeus was masterminding the whole racket. In calling him down from the tree, Jesus is engineering a meeting between Zacchaeus and the people he has wronged. Initially, the crowd is outraged with Jesus for befriending a man whose behaviour has spread fear and mistrust even amongst those he hasn't stolen from directly. And who can blame them?[86]

As my world and law firm dissembled in the summer of 1997, I received an offer from my law school to teach pre-trial civil litigation.

I mentioned the offer to Jack who scoffed and said: "Oh, no. You're done. You're damaged goods." I declined the law school offer stating I had some looming disciplinary matters that could embarrass the law school. I felt like damaged goods.

---

[86] Booth, Cherie (2007). Themes of Restorative Justice Found in the Story of Zacchaeus In Justice Reflections: Worldwide Papers Linking Christian Ideas with Matters of Justice. Lincoln UK: Diocese of Lincoln, Issue 16 JR 118.

I told Mike Coffield about the law school's offer and Jack's epithet. Without hesitation Mike said: "in about 15 years you'll be a professor of ethics or criminal justice." That sounded like an appealing pipe dream.

With "damaged goods" comments like Jack's, I felt as welcome in my communities as Zachhaeus.[87] Yet, despite my reverse-Groucho cynicism for such a bold notion of my entry to a club like academe, Mike reminded me he had software pirating, hacking and identity theft clients whom he'd successfully placed in software development and computer security jobs after their release from the criminal justice system. Mike always spoke of such a return to the community as "a return to make good."

---

[87] While the story of Zaccheus may be a "Christian story," there is nothing inherently Christian about restorative justice. The "prime directive" in Judiasm to heal the world is "Tikkun Olam," which is inherently restorative. *See* Rabbi Geoffrey A. Mitelman, "Retributive Justice and Restorative Justice, Huffington Post, May 3, 2011 (The Talmud (Sanhedrin 65b) insists responsibility for healing is in our hands, if only we could overcome our own limitations: "Raba said: If the righteous desired it, they could be creators of worlds, as it is written, "But your iniquities have separated between you and your God [Isaiah 59:2].") http://www.huffingtonpost.com/rabbi-geoffrey-a-mitelman/retributive-justice-and-r_b_857219.html

A popular, current illustration of Mike's notion that lawbreakers can return to make good is Frank W. Abagnale Jr. (not Mike's client), recently a keynote speaker at the Financial Planning Association's 2011 annual conference. Abagnale is the grifter whose real life story is profiled in the feature film "Catch Me If You Can," directed by Steven Spielberg, and a current Broadway musical of that name. Abignale is now a security and financial fraud consultant.[88]

When Mike spoke of my "return to make good," he never used the terms "social justice," "restorative justice" or "civic engagement." He never discussed the concept of returning a lawbreaker to do good in the community he or she harmed as part of a criminal sentence.

But I know social and restorative justice, and civic engagement were in Mike's heart. Otherwise, he would not have been so eager to help me and predict or encourage my future as a professor.

---

[88] "Catch Me If You Can" Scam Artist Gives Ethics Advice To Advisors, Financial Advisor (September 16, 2011). http://www.fa-mag.com/fa-news/8551-financial-advisors-treat-your-client-like-you-would-wanted-to-be-treated-yourself-says-former-professional-con-man-.html

Simply, Mike started the work of my restoration. It's more than "recovery" or "rehabilitation," which is why "restoration," especially in terms of social justice seems to me so much more an apt term.

Mike also reminded me I had a soul. He showed me the power of immediate accountability when through the story and example of Iran-Contra rogue Major General Richard Secord, he suggested I voluntarily relinquish my law license, turn myself in to the State's Attorney, and testify if necessary without the Fifth Amendment or attorney-client privileges, and without any immunity if offered. Mike got me thinking about voodoo ethics, even though he didn't call it that.

I've tried to stay on the path Mike showed me - to restoration - for the last 15 years. If I have any clear answers, they lay in the foundations of social and restorative justice, where the study of restoration as a path toward the best possible "wholeness" for victims and lawbreakers has currency beyond currency itself.

As I stated in the Introduction to this book, for me social justice is about creating meaningful education and employment opportunities, i.e., real second chances, for people who earned and deserve them; it's not about creating entitlements and fiscal burdens no one can afford.

For people with criminal records this means leveling the education and employment playing fields so most of this nearly one-third of America can get back to sustainable work. America has 5 percent of the world's population, 25 percent of the world's prisoners, nearly 2.4 million people incarcerated, the world's highest incarceration rate and approximately 7 million people under correctional supervision.[89]

It is no surprise academe has begun formally to study sentiments for radical change in the criminal justice system. One survey found that 75% of Americans were in favor of "totally revamping the way the criminal justice system works."[90]

Too many people are compromised or harmed regularly by a criminal justice system's "corrective" arm that fails to yield a corrective outcome.[91]   Former prisoners have greater

---

[89] *Supra*, at 23, 25-26.

[90] Heather Strang and Lawrence W. Sherman, The Practice of Restorative Justice: Repairing the Harm: Victims and Restorative Justice 2003 UTAH L. REV. 15 (citing John M. Boyle, CRIME ISSUES IN THE NORTHEAST 1 (1999).

[91] Lawbreakers' wages tend to be lower than what he or she earned before committing a crime. *See* Richard B. Freeman, Crime and the Employment of Disadvantaged Youth, in URBAN LABOR MARKETS

chances than not, of recidivism,[92] i.e., reoffending
and returning to custody.[93] Without education
and employment, odds are generally that two out
of three or more people with a felony conviction
will reoffend.[94]

AND JOB OPPORTUNITY 201, 234–35 (George Peterson
& Wayne Vronman eds., 1992) (finding that young
men who have been incarcerated do not do well on job
market years into future when compared to their own
pre-prison employment record.); *See also* Austin, J.,
Marino, B. A., Carroll, L., McCall, P. L., & Richards,
S. C. (2001). The Use of Incarceration in the United
States: National Policy White Paper. Washington,
DC: American Society of Criminology.
http://www.ssc.wisc.edu/-oliver/RACIAL/Reports/asci
ncarcerationdraft.pdf; Samuel L. Myers, Jr., Do Better
Wages Reduce Crime?, American Journal of
Economics and Sociology, Vol. 43, No. 2 (Apr. 1984),
191-195.

[92] "Recidivism is the return of a criminal to crime
within a specified time interval after release from
prison or completion of a punishment for a prior
conviction." Telidevara, S. (2010). In Morgan P. (Ed.),
Essays on recidivism, p.2. United States -- New York:
Economics.http://search.proquest.com/docview/759413
499?accountid=28180.

[93] "State Rates of Incarceration by Race," 2004; Sabol,
Minton & Harrison, 2007; "The Disaster Center,"
2010).

[94] *See* State of Recidivism: The Revolving Door of
America's Prisons, April 2011. A report from the Pew
Center on the States, provides national and state-level
data on offenders released from and returned to
prison.http://www.pewcenteronthestates.org/uploaded
Files/Pew_State_of_Recidivism.pdf

*   *

The "social justice" solution to our plague of over-incarceration, widespread recidivism and mass unemployment of people with criminal records is education and civic engagement in one form or another. It has nothing to do with more government or higher taxes or spending.

In *Politics*, Aristotle said, "Every state is a community of some kind, and every community is established with a view to some good; ...[95]

In "How to Talk Well," James Bender tells of a farmer who grew award-winning ribbon corn. A reporter interviewed the farmer and learned his secret. The reporter was surprised to discover the farmer shared his seed corn with his neighbors.

"How can you afford to share your best seed corn with your neighbors when they are entering corn in competition with yours each year?" the reporter asked.

"Why sir," said the farmer, "didn't you know? The wind blows pollen from the ripening corn and swirls it from field to field. If my neighbors grow inferior corn, cross-pollination will steadily

---

[95] Aristotle, and Benjamin Jowett. 1943. Aristotle's Politics. New York: Modern library.

degrade my corn. If I am to grow good corn, I
must help my neighbors grow good corn."[96]

Through civic engagement, white-collars can be
teachers and corn farmers.[97] To avoid cross-
pollination from the inferior corn lurking in the
criminal justice system and the bad seeds of post-
incarceration unemployment and discrimination,
policy-makers should consider mandating the
teaching of "other-collars" by white-collars. [98]

---

[96] Bender, James F. How to Talk Well. New York:
McGraw-Hill, 1949.

[97] Civically engaged activity can also include service
learning, philanthropy and work in the non-profit
sector, trusteeship, membership in civic associations,
social or military service, political participation,
registering to vote, and voting. *See, e.g.,* Preface, The
Civically Engaged Reader, The Great Books
Foundation (Chicago 2006).

[98] My term "other-collar" is intentional and somewhat
a euphemism for the disproportionate incarceration
of minorities, which is itself a vast subject and focus of
substantial academic work. And these indeed are a
vast populous of minds it would be terrible to waste.
See, e.g., Alexander, Michelle. 2010. The new Jim
Crow: mass incarceration in the age of colorblindness.
New York: New Press; and Prof. Glenn Toury
(Lecture) "Ghettos, Prisons and Racial Stigma," April
4, 2007
http://www.econ.brown.edu/fac/glenn_loury/louryhom
epage/teaching/ec%20137/ec%20137%20spring07/lectu
re%20i.pdf.

The Preface and Introduction to the book "Civic Responsibility and Higher Education"[99] contains two useful definitions:

> Civic engagement means working to make a difference in the civic life of our communities and developing the combination of knowledge, skills, values and motivation to make that difference. It means promoting the quality of life in a community, through both political and non political processes.

- Preface, page vi

> A morally and civically responsible individual recognizes himself or herself as a member of a larger social fabric and therefore considers social problems to be at least partly his or her own; such an individual is willing to see the moral and civic dimensions of issues, to make and justify informed moral and civic judgments, and to take action when appropriate.

- Introduction, page xxvi

For a discussion of this topic in terms of restorative justice, see generally, Raye, Barbara (2004). How Do Culture, Class and Gender Affect the Practice of Restorative Justice? (Part 2) In, Howard Zehr and Barb Toews, eds., Critical Issues in Restorative Justice. Monsey, New York and Cullompton, Devon, UK: Criminal Justice Press and Willan Publishing. Pp. 325-336.

[99] Ehrlich, Thomas. 2000. Civic responsibility and higher education. Phoenix, Az: Oryx Press.

Civic engagement can empower the millions of minds that have so much good seed corn to spread, even if in the eyes of other people our criminal records make us "damaged goods."

If policy-makers don't view advancing the common good with good seed through civic engagement as the mission critical element in restoring our criminal justice system, we will simply make things worse with more of the same. In this sense "social justice" is bi-partisan, because it is good business and inherently restorative.

My dear late friend, Jeff Paige, to whom this book is dedicated in loving memory, was a superb corn farmer. He always said in his work helping other people: "if you always do what you've always done, you'll always get what you've always got."

Restorative justice principles offer a key context and avenue for implementing education policies and civic engagement activities, which together can revamp our broken system, so we don't do what we've always done: waste so many minds.

It boils down to our willingness to view civic engagement strategies as a relatively inexpensive, if not essentially free, method of reversing the spillage our criminal justice system has allowed and continues to seep into our communities.

In a "macro" sense, civic engagement can be as to restoration of harm from our present criminal justice system as eradication of DDT was from agriculture, trans fats from grocery shelves, or removal of words like "Negro" from the lexicon.

In a "micro" sense, civic engagement can be as to restoring individual felons to active, productive lives as was progressing from the use of leeches to blood transfusions.

Civic engagement is our best tool for the restorative justice toolbox.

N.B.: As my context is white-collar crime, where so often no amount of money can restore one or many victims, the thrust of my discussion and analysis is how civic engagement can be used to empower people with criminal records to restore communities, rather than individual victims.

If in the process of any one felon's individual restoration, reentry, recovery or rehabilitation, that person can restore a victim monetarily, somewhat or in large part, that is of course crucial. But in the context of white-collar crime, as I said in the Introduction and Reflections, advancing the common good in a sense must eclipse individual recompense or the mistaken Holy Grail of just one person's "wholeness."

1. The Restorative Justice Toolbox, in Context and Defined

A pioneer scholar in restorative justice, Howard Zehr, gives meaning and purpose for the application of restorative justice principles:

> crime is a violation of people and relationships. It creates obligations to make things right. Justice involves the victim, the offender, and the community in a search for solutions which promote repair, reconciliation, and reassurance.[100]

One of many useful definitions for "restorative justice:"

> Restorative justice is a way of seeing crime as more than breaking the law – it also causes harm to people, relationships, and the community. So a just response must address those harms as well. If they are willing, the best way to do this is for the parties themselves to meet to discuss the harms and how to about bring resolution. (Other approaches are available if they are unable or unwilling to meet.)

---

[100] Changing Lenses: A New Focus for Crime and Justice. Scottsdale, Pennsylvania; Waterloo, Ontario: Herald Press, 1990. p 181.

Sometimes those meetings lead to transformational changes in their lives."[101]

John Braithwaite, perhaps more a restorative justice fundamentalist[102] than I am, defines the philosophy of the restorative justice movement as "healing rather than hurting, moral learning, community participation and community caring, respectful dialogue, forgiveness, responsibility, apology, and making amends."[103]

---

[101] Restorative Justice Online, Lecture Hall, Lesson 1: http://www.restorativejustice.org/university-classroom/01introduction/tutorial-introduction-to-restorative-justice/lesson-1-definition/lesson-1-definition

[102] John Braithwaite, A Future Where Punishment Is Marginalized, Realistic or Utopian?, 46 UCLA L. REV. 1727 (1999).

[103] John Braithwaite, Restorative Justice: Assessing Optimistic and Pessimistic Accounts, 25 CRIME & JUST. 1, 6 (1999)

Restorative justice is not, however, a sole
messianic, criminal justice paradigm changer. But
it does improve the *status quo* and advance the
common good, because it creates no additional
social costs while failing to deter crime. Plus, as I
say elsewhere, restorative justice better reduces
recidivism more so than pure punishment.[104]

Restorative justice practices in the U.S. (and
worldwide) are presently applied mostly in local
criminal justice systems, commonly to juvenile
crime, adult crime property crime and to violent
crime.[105, 106]

---

[104] *Supra*, n. 92-94.

[105] As of approximately 2007, there were over 300
restorative justice programs in almost every state. See
Patrick Glen Drake, Victim-Offender Mediation in
Texas: "When Eye for Eye" Becomes "Eye to Eye," 47
S. TEX. L. REV. 647, 668-669 (2006).

[106] According to the National Survey of Victim-
Offender Mediation in the United States, the four
most common offenses in the survey's programs are
vandalism, minor assaults, theft, and burglary. See
Mark S. Umbreit & Jean Greenwood (Apr. 2000)
National Survey of Victim-Offender Mediation The
truth is most makers of law and policy have it
backwards: punishment alone deters little and in
common terms, we have made a mess of our criminal
justice system because we belabor the tired notion of
punishment in a vacuum. Programs in the United
States, U.S. DEPARTMENT OF JUSTICE, OFFICE OF
JUSTICE PROGRAMS, Office for Victims of Crime, at
7.

Restorative justice has even recently become a campaign buzzword for aspiring prosecutors in the context of juvenile and violent crimes.[107]

However, restorative practices are less frequently applied to white-collar crime because most policy makers and prosecutors are with some – but not entirely – reasonable basis likely concerned that restorative practices to white-collar crime would challenge dominant utilitarian punishment theories and thus they question its legitimacy.

---

[107] "Prosecutor Candidates Support 'Restorative Justice'," September 18, 2011, New York Times, http://www.nytimes.com/2011/09/18/us/prosecutor-candidates-support-restorative-justice.html?_r=1

Prosecutors well recognize the bigger the crime the harder compensation for victims becomes, so maybe they suspect restorative justice just won't work. [108],[109]

I think it will work if we don't make pure "wholeness" *the* Holy Grail, but rather include restorative elements in traditional punishments.

"Very whole enough" is "very good enough." And very whole enough is a far better common good than not whole at all or barely whole, which too frequently has been our path in criminal justice.

---

[108] Utilitarian punishment theory holds that criminal sanctions are warranted primarily if they benefit society, because they deter lawbreakers and others from committing future crimes. Zvi D. Gabbay, *supra* at no. 21-23, "Holding Restorative Justice Accountable," citing JEREMY BENTHAM, AN INTRODUCTION TO THE PRINCIPLES OF MORALS AND LEGISLATION 165 (J.H. Burns & H.L.A. Hart eds., 1982) (1783), and Eric Luna, Punishment Theory, Holism, and the Procedural Conception of Restorative Justice, 2003 UTAH L. REV. 205, 208-9 (2003) (reviews basic utilitarian punishment theory, adds some distinct utilitarian goals like rehabilitation and incapacitation to deter crime).

[109] This is a predominant theme and message in Zvi D. Gabbay, *supra* at no. 21-23, "Holding Restorative Justice Accountable."

Importantly, a restorative program's rationale is not to be kind or compassionate to lawbreakers. Rather, it's a public policy acknowledgement that the social and economic cost of saddling certain white-collars (and other-collars) with lifelong felon brands is too high. No one can afford it; not victims, families, state human services departments that make welfare payments to indigent parents or that pay state-funded health insurance, and not prison budgets.

This is why restorative justice should function as one key – but not an exclusive – structural response to white-collar crime. More effectively than simply punishment, it can still provide traditional deterrents like incarceration, fines, personal shame and public opprobrium but together with a component that addresses crime-created needs and how to repair the harm.[110]

---

[110] *See, e.g.*, Dan M. Kahan & Eric A. Posner, Shaming White-Collar Criminals: A Proposal for Reform of the Federal Sentencing Guidelines, 42 J.L. & ECON. 365, 367–68 (1999); Paul McCold, A Causal Theory of Restorative Justice, Paper presented at THE 7TH INTERNATIONAL CONFERENCE ON CONFERENCING, CIRCLES, AND OTHER RESTORATIVE PRACTICES, Manchester, England, Nov. 2005, cited in Zvi D. Gabbay, EXPLORING THE LIMITS OF THE RESTORATIVE JUSTICE PARADIGM: RESTORATIVE JUSTICE AND WHITE-COLLAR CRIME Spring, 2007, 8 Cardozo J. Conflict Resol. 421, at n. 21.

As I demonstrate, we can infuse in our criminal justice and legal profession disciplinary responses, solutions that are *both* retributive "just desserts" and that assure punishments fit the crime, but that fit because they advance the common good; not because the severity of punishment meets the severity of the crime or transgression.

Eyes for eyes are dangerous because when it's all over, everyone's vision is worse. Punishment that focuses on severity of the crime without also "making things better" does not advance the common good, which advancement is - for me – the highest best application of restorative justice principles.

Theoretically, restorative justice solutions should focus on

 (i) Empowering victim reparation if possible (restitution);

 (ii) Reconciliation if the lawbreaker and victim are willing, and

(iii) Solutions that can heal or benefit the community in which a crime occurred – when possible. [III]

Practically speaking, however, the law must catch up with current thinking, learning and practice in the restorative justice field. Some of the reported opinions that discuss restoration seem to be overly punishment-oriented to the point of dismissing victim restoration outright.

The court decisions that follow illustrate my view that generally, our courts seem to have rejected outright the notion that restoration is at all or should be a state or governmental function.

[III] *See*, Zvi D. Gabbay, EXPLORING THE LIMITS OF THE   RESTORATIVE   JUSTICE   PARADIGM: RESTORATIVE JUSTICE AND WHITE-COLLAR CRIME, Spring, 2007, 8 Cardozo J. Conflict Resol. 421, n. 23: "The concept of 'community' in the restorative justice paradigm has various different meanings and roles. In discussing these different meanings, Paul McCold distinguishes between "local communities" and "personal communities," defined as "individuals who know and are personally involved in the lives of the victim and/or the offender." Paul McCold, Restorative Justice: The Role of the Community, Paper presented to THE ACADEMY OF CRIMINAL JUSTICE SCIENCES ANNUAL CONFERENCE, Boston, MA, Mar. 1995, http://www.restorativepractices.org/library/communit y3.html.

These court decisions are prime examples and compelling arguments as to why we need substantial public policy recognition of restorative justice principles and particularly for white-collars.

*   *

2. Restorative Justice at Law (Currently)

The United Supreme Court and most federal courts of appeal have made clear in an unwittingly wrongheaded way that our criminal justice system is indeed essentially punitive and not restorative.

The distinctions between punishment and restoration expressed by the Supreme Court in the cases I discuss, and by lower courts in similar cases, do not reflect current learning or the reality of our failed criminal justice system. I offer these examples as arguments for the proposition that we can't do much worse than we have already, so how can infusion of restorative principles to white-collar and other crime fail more than traditional punishment schema as shown by our obscene incarceration and recidivism statistics?

In Kelly v. Robinson, 479 US 36 (1986), the United Supreme Court reviewed a Connecticut restitution statute to determine whether a restitution order was dischargeable in bankruptcy.

Granted, most people would have a negative visceral reaction as to whether a criminal defendant should be permitted to discharge a restitution order in a bankruptcy. So did the Supreme Court.

However, in explaining its rationale for saying, essentially, "never, except in rare circumstances," the Supreme Court's language can be read also to exclude reparations for victims as the concern of the criminal justice system; that punishment for the lawbreaker is really the only concern. Thus, while the Court can be said to have reached the correct ethical or moral decision, it's arguably for very wrong reasons.

The Court held that restitution granted in a state proceeding as a condition of probation could not be discharged because it constituted a criminal penalty enforced "for the benefit of" *the government* and did not serve primarily as "compensation for actual pecuniary loss" to *the victim* under § 523(a)(7) of the bankruptcy code.[112]

Initially the Court observed that "[t]he criminal justice system is not operated primarily for the benefit of victims."[113] The Court then stated that "[a]lthough restitution does resemble a judgment `for the benefit of' the victim," it is imposed in the context of a criminal sentence and "[t]he victim has no control over the amount ... or the decision to award" restitution.[114]

---

[112] 479 US at 43-53.

[113] *Id.*, at 52.

[114] *Id.*

Additionally, the Court said "the decision to impose restitution generally does not turn on the victim's injury, but on the penal goals of the state and the situation of the defendant."[115] Quoting the Bankruptcy Judge who decided the underlying issue, the Court finally observed that

> [u]nlike an obligation which arises out of a contractual, statutory or common law duty, here the obligation is rooted in the traditional responsibility of a state to protect its citizens by enforcing its criminal statutes and *to rehabilitate an offender by imposing a criminal sanction intended for that purpose.*[116]

(emphasis added).

Maybe in the mid-1980's when Kelly v. Robinson crawled through the court system, then current learning suggested more so than today that imposing a criminal sanction rehabilitates the lawbreaker. We now know with recidivism rates sometimes approaching 70%, that criminal sanctions alone are not such reliable tools for rehabilitation.[117]

---

[115] *Id.*

[116] *Id.*

[117] *See supra* at n.94, State of Recidivism: The Revolving Door of America's Prisons, April 2011.

The Supreme Court's view of restitution as punitive, and not restorative, is the same even when the Court has addressed restitution in contexts other than the well-intended prevention of a bankruptcy discharge of a restitution order.

More recently, the Supreme Court has still missed the opportunity to reflect current academic learning based on known data about the criminal justice system failures.

In Pasquantino v. United States, 544 US 349 (2005), writing for the majority Justice Clarence Thomas got it really wrong as indicated by his rather tired and dated espousal of the purposes for and effects of restitution.

Pasquantino was a wire fraud case in which the lawbreaker was a tax cheat; the Canadian government was the victim. The issue in the case involved application of the Mandatory Victims Restitution Act (the "MVRA"), and the Witness and Victim Protections Act ("WVPA").

Justice Thomas expressed the supposed public policy foundations for restitution distinctly as a criminal punishment, regardless of and ignoring any restorative purposes of these two statutes.

> We do not think it matters whether the provision of restitution is mandatory in this prosecution ... The purpose of awarding restitution in this action is not to collect a foreign tax, but *to mete out appropriate criminal punishment* for that conduct.

(emphasis added).

Justice Thomas here misses the point that restitution is to restore the victim. The punishment is the criminal sentence itself, i.e., prison or probation.

It's not that Justice Thomas is intellectually dishonest in this 2005 opinion, when perhaps we'd expect more current learning to reflect in a Supreme Court opinion. Rather, Justice Thomas is doing his job, more or less, as he has much jurisprudential company in this mistaken view, indicating more than anything how the law lags behind learning.

Restorative purpose in the criminal justice system is just not yet an idea whose time has fully come at the federal level. The Third, Fifth, Eighth, Ninth, Eleventh and D.C. Circuits all hold that restitution, when ordered in connection with a criminal conviction, is not to benefit the victim but instead is a criminal penalty.[118]

That's backwards; especially when our statistics indicate that punishment for punishment's sake leads to more punishment and the world's highest incarceration and recidivism rates.

---

[118] *See* United States v. Leahy et. al, 428 F3d 328 (3rd Cir. 2005) rehearing en banc (2006)(for purposes of Sixth Amendment fact-finding, restitution is a criminal penalty."); United States v. Rico Indus., Inc., 854 F.2d 710, 714 (5th Cir.1988) ("Restitution is a criminal penalty."); United States v. Williams, 128 F.3d 1239, 1241 (8th Cir.1997) ("We conclude an order of restitution under the MVRA is punishment for Ex Post Facto Clause purposes."); United States v. Miguel, 49 F.3d 505, 509 (9th Cir.1995) ("The [VWPA] also clearly indicates that restitution is a penalty available to sentencing courts regardless of other criminal penalties that may be imposed."); Creel v. Comm'r of Internal Revenue, 419 F.3d 1135, 1140 (11th Cir.2005) ("[A]n order to pay restitution under 18 U.S.C. § 3663 [the VWPA] is a criminal penalty rather than a civil penalty."); United States v. Bapack, 129 F.3d 1320, 1327 n. 13 (D.C.Cir.1997) (endorses Second Circuit's approach in Thompson).

Of the federal courts of appeal that have addressed whether restitution is punitive or restorative, only the Seventh and Tenth Circuits have held that restitution is a civil rather than a criminal penalty, i.e., not only punishment but also a remedy for the benefit of the victim.[119]

Victim-focused public policy is less bleak in the states than in the federal judiciary. Victims' advocacy groups have passed an array of legislation, which generally give victims rights to be notified at key procedural stages, and to be heard at defendants' sentencing hearings.[120]

---

[119] *See* United States v. Newman, 144 F. 3rd 531, 542 542 (7th Cir.1998) ("restitution authorized by the VWPA (and mandatorily imposed under the MVRA) is not a criminal punishment for purposes of the Ex Post Facto Clause"); United States v. Nichols, 169 F.2d 1255, 1279-80 (10th Cir. 1999) (adopts Seventh Circuit's Newman holding).

[120] *See* 91 A.L.R.5th 343 § 2[a] ("[A]lmost all states have enacted a wide variety of constitutional and statutory provisions[...under the rubric of victims' rights, which clauses have often been enacted by wide majorities." (citations omitted)).

Specifically as to restorative justice legislation for juveniles, there were as of 2007, 300 restorative justice programs nationwide, and as of 2008, sixteen states had enacted restorative justice legislation.[121]

It's no accident there are numerous state statutes mandating restorative justice schemes in one form or another, at least for juveniles. Studies indicate that application of restorative justice principles can reduce recidivism at higher rates than retributive models.[122]

---

[121] *See* Sandra Pavelka O'Brien (2008). Restorative Juvenile Justice Legislation and Policy: A National Assessment International Journal of Restorative Justice. 4(2): 100-118.

[122] *See, e.g.*, de Beus K., Rodriguez N. Restorative justice practice: An examination of program completion and recidivism (2007) Journal of Criminal Justice, 35 (3), pp. 337-347;   Restorative Justice Consortium, (2006) The Positive Effect of Restorative Justice on Re-offending, http://www.bristol-mediation.org/wp-content/uploads/2011/03/The-Positive-Effect-of-Restorative-Justice-on-Reoffending.pdf; Mark S. Umbreit, Betty Vos, Robert B. Coates, & Elizabeth Lightfoot, Symposium: Restorative Justice in Action: Restorative Justice in the Twenty-First Century: A Social Movement Full of Opportunities and Pitfalls, 89 Marq. L. Rev. 251, 284-289 (2005) (citing numerous meta-analyses which show reduced recidivism rates for restorative justice procedures). See also Jennifer Shack, Bibliographic Summary of Cost, Pace, and Satisfaction Studies of Court-Related Mediation Programs (Center for Analysis of Alternative Dispute

For example, a University of Pennsylvania meta-analysis of 11 studies showed recidivism was 27 percent lower among restorative justice participants than among defendants not involved in the program.[123]

Even if an argument can be made that white-collar recidivism is generally lower than in the general lawbreaker population, it doesn't make the argument for application of restorative justice principles to white-collar crime less compelling. Especially not when restorative justice offers reparative opportunities for the community that transcend prevention of recidivism.

*   *

Resolution System 2003); Latimer, J., Dowden, C., and Muise, D. The Effectiveness of Restorative Justice Practices: A Meta-Analysis. The Prison Journal 2005; 85; 127; Latimer, J., Dowden, C., and Muise, D. (2001). The Effectiveness of Restorative Justice Practices: A Meta-Analysis. Researchand Statistics Division, Department of Justice, Ottawa, Canada.

[123] "Prisoners Give Back to Society, Restorative justice programs pare recidivism," Southeast Missourian. May 18, 2011. http://www.columbiatribune.com/news/2011/may/18/pr isoners-give-back-to-society/

3.   **Rationales and Proposals for White-Collar Restorative Solutions**

Our traditional, utilitarian notions of retribution might be more justifiable if when the punishment ends we are willing to view the punished - who have paid their dues - as we view other poor, vulnerable, under-privileged populations.   But that's not what we do. Instead, we exile people with criminal records with our discriminatory laws and policies. That's why restorative justice and civic engagement are so needed as a sword and shield.

For all but the criminal class, we Judeo-Christians well understand how civic engagement can revitalize those in need. In Christian vernacular, we teach the hungry to fish. In Judaism, the highest degree of giving (a fundamental act of civic engagement) is to "uphold the hand of an Israelite reduced to poverty by handing him a gift or a loan, or entering into a partnership with him, or finding work for him in order to strengthen his hand, so that he would have no need to beg from other people."[124]

---

[124] Moses Maimonides, "Gifts to the Poor," Book Seven (The Book of Agriculture), Mishneh Torah.

With rare exception incarceration and criminal records are lifelong income retardants. Discrimination against us is legal, pretty much.[125]

So, if as a community, voters and policy-makers wish to be intellectually honest regarding the 91 million American's we've branded with criminal records, what must we confront?

On the "back end" of the criminal justice system, which begins upon conviction, we have little choice but to apply the highest form of ethics and social safety net consciousness when we stroke our chins wondering how to retread lawbreakers and get us back to work.

---

[125] Employment barriers and legal discrimination against felons is a vast body of work that exceeds my scope here. Recently, I've addressed these topics elsewhere in "MOVING THE BOX" BY EXECUTIVE ORDER IN ILLINOIS | De Paul Journal for Social Justice, 4 DePaul J. for Soc. Just. 1:17 Fall 2010. (with co-author Melissa McClure); BLUEPRINT FOR PROGRESS: HOW ILLINOIS EMPOWERS REHABILITATED PEOPLE WITH CRIMINAL RECORDS | Ch. 8, ISSUES WITH CRIMINAL RECORDS, 2010 Supplement, Illinois Institute of Continuing Legal Education | SUMMER 2010; BEYOND LEGAL MECHANISMS – EMPLOYMENT, HOUSING AND OTHER SUPPORTS | Ch. 6, ISSUES WITH CRIMINAL RECORDS, 2010 Supplement, Illinois Institute of Continuing Legal Education | SUMMER 2010 (with co-author, Jodina Hicks).

That's why I asked this question in the beginning of this book:

Do we want educated and capable white-collars costing taxpayers money while socially unproductive in prison cells or unemployed, or civically engaged, and working to help heal the communities we harmed, especially when restorative justice practices have been shown to reduce recidivism?

Crude evidence of our generally entrenched retributive practices makes the point: The annual cost to Michigan taxpayers to incarcerate one person is $35,000.[126] That's more than it costs to educate a University of Michigan student.[127]

---

[126] Hard dollar federal incarceration costs, without factoring in recidivism and external social costs, have been estimated at $20-$26,000-$30,000 annually. *See* Nkechi Taifa, "Three-Strikes-and-You're-Out"— Mandatory Life Imprisonment for Third Time Felons, 20 U. DAYTON L. REV. 717, 722 (1995); COOTER & ULEN, *supra* note 28, at 468.

[127] States Help Ex-Inmates Find Jobs
http://www.nytimes.com/2011/01/25/business/25offend er.html?_r=3&pagewanted=all

Maybe this sounds smug, but in a sense we're better off sending appropriate low level or first time lawbreakers to college *as part of their criminal sentences*, or spending sums like this on retreading white-collars or simply more educated lawbreakers to be educators and practitioners of civic engagement.[128]

This is not to say economic efficiency suggests we should imprison only the poor and otherwise punish white-collars, since imprisonment is so expensive why waste imprisonment dollars on good minds.[129] The point is we have egalitarian

---

[128] To carry the thought further toward a possibly logical extreme: if compassion for criminals or subsidizing our restoration with tax-payer money seems intellectually challenging, consider the maximum Pell Grant (for which felons are no longer eligible) is $5,550, and it costs an average of $26,-$35,000 to detain a prisoner each year. *Id.*, at n. 126. Rational policy-makers or tax-payers should readily trade an annual Pell Grant for four years of college for a felon to avoid having to fund the 68 percent-likelihood of multi-year recidivist prison stays. Before 1994 when Congress outlawed Pell Grants for felons, only one-tenth of one percent of Pell Grant funds went to felon students. Re-legalizing Pell Grants for felons is not only a good idea, it would be a fundamental act of restorative justice and civic engagement.

[129] This very real problem (not necessarily driven by economic efficiency concerns) arises in the context of mass or disproportionate sentencing of minorities, addressed in recent works like Michelle Alexander's "The New Jim Crow," *supra* at n. 98.

alternatives such as restorative justice, for which there is precedent for its application to white-collar crime.

John Braithwaite, to whom I referred earlier as a "restorative justice fundamentalist" has argued that restorative justice principles are already in use in many other countries to regulate corporate, white-collar conduct.[130]

Restorative solutions can be crafted for infusion in white-collar criminal sentences that should accomplish two goals:

(1) Part of the criminal sentence should redeploy (not necessarily or immediately *re-employ*) appropriate lawbreakers for the advancement of the common good in a role that uses the lawbreaker's brains or skill to effect reparations (even if it takes a lifetime), and fix or ameliorate pieces of the systemic problem (if identifiable) that allowed the crime to occur.

---

[130] JOHN BRAITHWAITE, RESTORATIVE JUSTICE & RESPONSIVE REGULATION 16, 128 (Oxford University Press, 2002).

(2) Divert appropriate lawbreakers from traditional taxpayer-draining penal paths if this can be done without compromising (the least necessary) retributive and deterrence goals (no more no less).

*   *

Current illustrative evidence of elements in traditional sentencing, which combine restorative and traditional retributive elements that could be applied to white-collars can be seen in the following two examples (and there are many):

<u>Offender Initiative Probation or Deferred Sentencing</u>: The Cook County, Illinois (Chicago) State's Attorney that prosecuted me now has a program for select one-time, non-violent lawbreakers the end result of which is a dismissed felony charge.

While in the program's initial stages, it is aimed primarily at youth but it can be applied to white-collars and other adults.

In appropriate cases, the prosecutor and court can agree that upon completion of a rigorous probation sentence, full restitution to the victim, GED education when applicable, and other terms decided on a case-by-case basis, the defendant's felony charge is dismissed and there is no conviction record on the defendant's record.[131]

The ultimate purpose for Offender Initiative (sometimes known as or akin to "Deferred Sentencing") programs is so maybe without a post-sentence felony accompanying every employment application for the foreseeable future, the defendant can have some realistic chance at working at his or her pre-conviction level, or as to youth having a clean record, and some realistic possibilities for earning a living, supporting a family, etc.

---

[131] "Alvarez launches Offender Initiative Probation Program," Copyline News Magazine, March 12, 2011. http://www.copylinemagazine.com/news/2011/03/12/alvarez-launches-offender-initiative-probation-program/. The City of Bellevue, Washington has a very similar program. http://www.bellevuewa.gov/probation_services_programs.htm

<u>Public Speaking About an Offense</u>. In addition to fines and imprisonment, the former chief executive of the hedge fund Quellos Group, Jeffrey Greenstein, and former tax attorney Charles Wilk, were ordered by a US District Judge as a community service condition of their criminal sentence resulting from a tax shelter fraud, to return to their respective alma maters, the University of Washington Foster Business School, and New York University Law School, to lecture on business and legal ethics.[132]

The foregoing examples are a glimpse of what is possible.

*   *

Following are three proposals fundamentally based in a convergence of economic efficiency and communitarian principles.

---

[132] "Ex-Chief of Quellos Admits Swindling the I.R.S. Out of $240 Million," New York Times, Sept 10, 2010.http://www.nytimes.com/2010/09/11/business/11h edge.html

The rationale: Rehabilitation through education of less educated lawbreakers, sometimes by more educated lawbreakers, can sufficiently increase the opportunity cost of crime so working in real jobs is attainable, more profitable and less risky.[133] Each proposal offers restorative and reparative opportunities for communities that could be institutionalized as part of white-collar sentences, either while a white-collar is incarcerated or as part of community service hour obligations while on probation. One proposal offers opportunities for fallen lawyers as well.

The proposed examples illustrate deployment of variously skilled white-collars to train "other-collar" in fields where a felony conviction least affects or impairs a felon's post-sentence future or pursuit of education and employment.

The three key examples are:

---

[133] See Josephine R. Potuto, The Modern Prison: Let's Make It a Factory for Change, 18 U. TOL. L. REV. 51, 56 (1986) ("The case for rehabilitation may be stated simply. It is clear that at least some criminals resort to crime for want of any better way to earn a living. Since providing the means and attitudes to be a success at employment reduces the need and, hence, the incentive, to commit crime, then providing employment training and saleable skills could assist released prisoners to avoid recidivating.")

(1) Require more educated lawbreakers to educate less educated lawbreakers, because education is the foundation for sustainable employment;

(2) Require white-collars with higher level business experience formally to teach entrepreneurship and business skills to other-collars whose offenses exhibit adept entrepreneurial skills, to promote self-initiated livelihoods rather than the dramatically less fruitful pursuit of traditional employment; and

(3) With redemptive *quid pro quo*, i.e., presumptive proof of rehabilitation for relicensing, state bar regulators should offer the opportunity and incentive for disbarred or suspended lawyers (hundreds to thousands annually), many of whom populate the criminal justice system, to work for a period of time, e.g., three to seven years, as lobbyists for nonprofit organizations with social justice missions.

Lobbying and advocacy is inherently a First Amendment activity, and thus essentially unregulated with almost no disqualifications, occupational bars or unauthorized practice of law sanctions that exclude disbarred lawyers or felons.

* *

a. **Education of the Less Educated by the More Educated**

"I ain't got time for school. I gotta work."

"Our funders don't pay for education; they pay for jobs."

I have heard both of these sentiments expressed to me in earnest and repeatedly by formerly incarcerated people with no education and no job, and worse yet by non-profit social service administrators (funded with at least as much public money as private money) who attempt to find jobs for formerly incarcerated people with little or no education. The reference is irresistible: "'No, no!' said the Queen. 'Sentence first -- verdict afterward.'" Only where non-profits meet the uneducated and unemployed would stewards of the public interest and public money emphasize work before education - with a straight face.

Outside of the criminal justice system, no one quarrels with the need for education of the less educated by the more educated. That's how ancient and modern cultures operate and have survived since culture emerged. Yet in our modern culture, when it comes to lawbreakers and education, we reverse or eschew all known models for cultural success and do everything that doesn't work. We exhibit a near pathological, exclusionary mindset that presumes once a lawbreaker becomes "damaged goods" all bets are off. We have implemented a generation of public policies that reject for lawbreakers myriad known solutions and proven, necessary social supports for all of us who haven't broken the law or who haven't been caught yet: e.g., education, student loans, decent housing, employment, health care, and the like.

Our failure to elevate education above incarceration, even for lawbreakers, manifests in the poorest communities that usually carry the weight of felon reentry with the most inadequate resources. The poor get poorer, but even more shameful the dumb get dumber, and then they and their children go to prison. And I don't mean unintelligent people. I'm speaking about, and for, people with little or no voice.

This persistent systemic problem in contemporary parlance is the "school-to-prison pipeline," the path driven by the policies and practices that push America's most at-risk (poorest and usually non-caucasian) school children, from school into the juvenile or criminal justice systems.

This pipeline reflects our elevation of incarceration over education.[134] And this will get worse in our foreseeable economic future if we don't treat the millions of minds we have locked up and wasting in corrections cycles as efficient, sustainable human capital that costs relatively little to train and deploy.

In Illinois, more than half of the approximately 40,000 people leaving Illinois prisons annually return to just seven (7) - and the poorest - of Chicago's 77 neighborhoods.[135] Of these 20,000 people approximately 6% end up homeless, as they do nationwide in approximately the same proportion.[136]

---

[134] *See* Locating the School-to-Prison Pipeline, ACLU factsheet.
http://www.aclu.org/files/images/asset_upload_file966_35553.pdf

[135] Rex W. Huppke, Ex-Cons Flock to 7 Areas in Chicago: Jobs Scarce, Crime Prevalent, Study Finds, Chicago Tribune, NNW Ed., Sept. 15, 2005, Metro Section, p. 4. http://articles.chicagotribune.com/2005-09-15/news/0509150222_1_prisoner-re-entry-ex-offenders-illinois-department.

[136] In a 36-city survey on hunger and homelessness, officials in six cities identified prison (Cleveland, Denver, New Orleans, Phoenix, Seattle, and Washington, DC) as a major contributor to homelessness. U.S. Conference of Mayors, A Status Report on Hunger and Homelessness in American Cities, pp. 82-83 (2002) (Washington, D.C. United States Conference of Mayors).

One "solution" cannot be, however, the one that pervades in bad economies: to throw our hands up because we don't have any more good money to throw at a chronically bad situation. Our response should be to identify deployable resources that lead to known solutions that don't cost vast sums of money we no longer have anyway.

The solution to ease the burden of felon reentry on the poorest communities is affordable education of inmates and especially all people exiting the criminal justice system. Education doesn't become *less* fundamental because someone breaks the law, gets caught and is convicted. It becomes *more* important, but our public policies don't suggest we actually believe as much.

The primary reason affordable education is the primary solution is not unique to lawbreakers or prisons. For all people, even lawbreakers, education is the foundation for sustainable employment (among other things).[137] So, for policy-makers and prison administrators, it should be old news or tautology that education is "one of the most productive and important

---

[137] A study conducted in Massachusetts indicates prisoners who had received some college education fared well. The reported results differ but make the point. *See* Eric Blumenson & Eva S. Nilsen, How to Construct an Underclass, or How the War on Drugs Became a War on Education, 6 J. GENDER RACE & JUST. 61, 79 n.91 (2002) (not one of several hundred prisoners in Massachusetts who received college degree was sent back toprison over twenty-five year period). *But see* Lisa Ouimet Burke and James E. Vivian, The Effect of College Programming on Recidivism Rates at the Hampden County House of Correction: a Five-Year Study. (prisoners who received some college education while incarcerated represented a recidivism rate of 46.8 percent, nearly one third below the state average.) http://www.stcloudstate.edu/continuingstudies/distanc e/documents/EffectofCollegeProgrammingonRecidivi smRatesattheHampdenCountyHouseofCorrectionA5 YearStudyBur.pdf

reentry services,"[138] and that employment reduces recidivism precipitously.[139]

Education for lawbreakers yields far lower recidivism rates, but most prisons have done precisely the opposite of what is most necessary in the worst economic times: cut education programs when even more money should be spent on them.

---

[138] Gaes, G. 2008. The impact of prison education on post-release outcomes. New York: John Jay College of Criminal Justice.
http://www.urban.org/projects/reentry-roundtable/upload/Gaes.pdf.

[139] It's a straightforward proposition. We reduce recidivism when we make the cost of crime high enough that the wages of gainful, legal employment look and are, in fact, better. *See, e.g.*, Samuel L. Myers, Jr., Estimating the Economic Model of Crime: Employment Versus Punishment Effects, 98 Q. J. ECON. 157, 157 (1983) (relationship between higher wages and reduced crime). *See also*, Marlaina Freisthler and Mark A. Godsey , GOING HOME TO STAY: A REVIEW OF COLLATERAL CONSEQUENCES OF CONVICTION, POST-INCARCERATION EMPLOYMENT, AND RECIDIVISM IN OHIO Spring, 2005 36 U. Tol. L. Rev. 525; Elena Saxonhouse, Note, Unequal Protection: Comparing Former Felons' Challenges to Disenfranchisement and Employment Discrimination, 56 STAN. L. REV. 1597, 1611 & n.79 (2004)(research indicates work reduces recidivism); Leroy D. Clark, A Civil Rights Task: Removing Barriers to Employment of Ex-Convicts, 38 U.S.F. L. REV. 193, 200-01 (1993) (unemployment strongly correlates with recidivism).

A 1997 study published by the Illinois Department of Corrections indicated that academic and vocational post-secondary education cut recidivism by two-thirds, from 39 percent to 13 percent. Similar outcomes pervade nationwide regardless of race, age, nature of offense, length of incarceration, for men and women.[140] Plus, most people value their education, including lawbreakers. In a recent evaluation and study, ninety-four percent of state and federal inmates interviewed before release consistently identified education as a personal reentry need. [141]

---

[140] "Cuts in Prison Education Put Illinois at Risk," John Howard Association of Illinois, May 2010.

[141] See, e.g., S.J. Steurer, J. Linton, J. Nally, and S. Lockwood, Top Nine Reasons to Increase Correctional Education Programs, August 2010, Corrections Today.(The Serious and Violent Offender Reentry Initiative evaluation documented 94 percent of state and federal inmates interviewed before releas identified education as a personal reentry need), http://www.ceanational.org/images/Steurer_August201 0-CT.PDF, citing Visher, C.A. and P.K. Lattimore. 2007. Major study examines prisoners and their reentry needs. NIJ Journal, 258:32. Washington D.C.: National Institute of Justice. http://www.ojp.usdoj.gov/nij/journals/258/reentry-needs.html

We really do hold the key to our own jail to solve the problem of funding education in prison and beyond. Appropriate white-collars under correctional supervision should educate "other-collars" in prison, on parole and probationers.

There are successful, scalable analog models for this that can be replicated with little cost. Two examples are the 20 year-old Changing Lives with Literature "bibliotherapy" program originated in Massachusetts,[142] and the ability of Chicago's 60-year old Great Books Foundation to implement its programs nationwide.[143]

Neither of these models presently utilize white-collars to educate other-collars, but they provide the base proof that such models can affordably fill the existing education gap in the criminal justice system. Both programs are uniquely suited for adaptation to include white-collars and other educated lawbreakers as instructors, teachers, tutors, mentors, and facilitators who work on behalf of the public as part of their own criminal

---

[142] Founded in 1991 by University of Massachusets Professor Robert Waxler and Judge Robert Kane http://cltl.umassd.edu/home-flash.cfm

[143] Philosopher Mortimer Adler and University of Chicago President Robert Maynard Hutchins founded the Great Books Foundation in 1947. http://GreatBooks.org

sentences. Theoretically, this concept should bother none of the pertinent stakeholders (except maybe teachers' unions).

(i) What is "Bibliotherapy" and What is it's Promise?

Despite that America has the most incarcerated people on earth, probation is our most common correctional disposition.[144] While standard probation does little to reduce recidivism,[145] "enhanced" probation programs can do so.

One such enhanced "bibliotherapy" program operates as an alternative sentencing program designed to reduce recidivism. Simply, "bibliotherapy" incorporates learning and rehabilitation through the use of literature study

---

[144] Glaze, Lauren E. Thomas P. Bonczar, and Fan Zhang. 2010. Probation and Parole in the United States, 2009. Washington, DC: Bureau of Justice Statistics. NCJ 231674 Bulletin, cited in Schutt, Russell K. Changing Lives Through Bibliotherapy and Recidivism Among Probationers. (July 12, 2011) SSRN. http://ssrn.com/abstract=1884659 ("Changing Lives").

[145] Green, Donald P. and Daniel Winik. 2010. Using Random Judge Assignments to Estimate the Effects of Incarceration and Probation on Recidivism among Drug Offenders. Criminology 48:357-387., cited in Changing Lives, at 4.

to develop and enhance crucial cognitive and critical thinking skills.

The "Changing Lives Through Literature" program began in the 1990s in Massachusetts and now operates in at least six states. On a one-court-at-a-time and one-judge-at-a-time basis, the program reduces probation sentences in exchange for participation in small book discussion groups that include probation officers and judges, as well as the student-probationers. The program is strictly an alternative sentencing program *for* probationers, but portends great success and alternative uses in general education *for and by* incarcerated and other lawbreakers.

Teaching a person to lead or facilitate literature discussion groups is not rocket science, nor is it expensive. With proper training, effective group leading comes from hands on learning by doing. The group leader's function is not to impart information didactically, but rather to fill a quasi-Socratic role. The skill of the facilitator unfolds in the asking of questions that advance the learning experience based on the subject texts.

As an economic proposition, training appropriate white-collars or other sufficiently literate lawbreakers to be "teachers" in such a program doesn't require an investment of many years or dollars, nor is this type of teacher's tool box filled

with facts, figures, lesson plans, quizzes, mid-
terms or final exams. This type of teacher's sole
arsenal is the combination of listening and
questioning skills. No teacher or student in such
a setting is there to ask objective questions or to
give right or wrong answers. The best questions
are entirely interpretive and the best answers are
only positions and perspectives that are well
supported by the readings.

This approach to learning and the acquired skill is
the type of critical thinking that frees most
people to succeed, because once a person can ask
good questions, the fewer facts and figures
anyone really needs "to know" and the more
aggressive in the pursuit of knowledge and
direction most people will be.

In his July 2011 study, "Changing Lives Through
Literature: Bibliotherapy and Recidivism among
Probationers," University   of Massachusetts
Professor   Russell   Schutt   and   colleagues
investigated the effect of the Changing Lives
Through Literature program on recidivism.[146]
This study compared 673 program participants in
five jurisdictions to a comparison sample of 1,574
non-program   probationers   in   the   same
jurisdictions.

---

[146] *Id.*, at n. 142.

Many program participants described their experience as transformative, the impact of which indicated a significant reduction in the pre-and-post program participation arrest rates. Similarly, if program participants reoffended at all, their offenses were not nearly as bad as other non-program probationers. Further, Professor Schutt's study suggests these declines were unrelated to background factors, drug use, and years of criminal history; and the declines in re-arrest rates were even more pronounced particularly for drug users and older probationers.

Professor Schutt's results suggest the importance of enhanced probation programs that advance cognitive change along with the establishment of new social relations for participating probationers.

But Schutt's results suggest something more profound and more sustainable than even enhanced probation programs: programs like Changing Lives Through Literature can provide a restorative framework and inexpensive venue for empowering white-collars to serve other-collars in education, and thereby to serve and advance the common good; not in lieu of punishment but as part of their criminal sentences.

In the same manner that program participants in Changing Lives can receive time reductions from their sentence, so too could and should potential white-collar group leaders and facilitators.

All this can be accomplished essentially by imparting listening and question-asking skills, which skills are taught, used in and define the more formally developed and proprietary Shared Inquiry™ method pioneered by Chicago's Great Books Foundation.

*   *

(ii) <u>What is Shared Inquiry and Why Can it Educate so Many Lawbreakers for So Little Money?</u>

Shared Inquiry is an essentially modified Socratic process that is far more developed doctrinally than it may be in the Changing Lives program. The branded, proprietary "Shared Inquiry" method has been in use by the Chicago-based Great Books Foundation for 60 years.

Shared Inquiry is elegantly simple. It's based on the asking of interpretive questions and answers supported by textual evidence. In short, that's it. My students respond with great enthusiasm when I tell them at the beginning of each semester that in my classes there are no correct answers; only well-supported ones based on evidence from the reading assignment. This is a gesture of respect when a teacher tells students they cannot be wrong. Shared Inquiry also requires no memorization. Shared Inquiry requires that students read, think, make notes, and read again before the group discussion convenes. Shared Inquiry invigorates students and frees them to think. Shared Inquiry allows the group access to the minds of the participants in a stress-free environment.

Shared Inquiry is perfect for security-conscious prisons, and any other aspect of the criminal justice system that has any type of equipment or technology limitations. Shared Inquiry requires no Internet, no smart classrooms, no laptop computers or e-learning platforms, nor even a blackboard or chalk. It requires only a trained group discussion leader, prepared group participants, and books. Traditionally, the Great Books Foundation has trained group leaders and has provided the books. Millions of adults and children have experienced Great Books, in both adult and Junior Great Books for children K-12.

The Institute for People with Criminal Records, of which I am Founder, has begun a Great Books in Prison program in the Illinois Department of Corrections' Dwight Correctional Facility for Women, in Dwight, Illinois. Initial results based on the feedback from Great Books personnel and prison personnel were beyond expectation and positive. We are pursuing additional collaborations to infuse Shared Inquiry-based programs to serve other demographics within the community of people with criminal records, such as probationers, restorative justice programs, children of incarcerated parents, and minors in the juvenile justice system.

Along the way in our integration of Shared Inquiry applications in the criminal justice world, we are seeking to groom willing and able lawbreaker participants as group leaders.[147]

A net result of policies and programs like Changing Lives Through Literature and the Great Books' Shared Inquiry method, both the type that can empower education of the less educated by the more educated is, to borrow from the modern sustainability lexicon, enhancement of the "triple bottom line," i.e., advancement of the common good with financial and social justice benefits:

---

[147] Such skills once imparted to white-collars or other collars for application in a book discussion group within prisons or probation departments don't invade the ambit of competition-phobic teachers' unions, because no one needs a license to listen and ask questions, and no prison or criminal justice administrators are so bound by union contracts. If they are, such contracts should be scrutinized when up for bargaining and renegotiation, and legislators can enact statutes that would mandate such programs outside the scope of what protections teachers' unions do have in existing contracts. Questions of union relationships and politics to prison budgets and programs are well covered in the academic literature and the media.

- Shorter and thus less expensive incarceration periods due to time reduction rewards for program participation;

- More educated other-collars whom are less likely to reoffend;

- More employable other-collars, because they would have critical thinking and liberal arts education (which cost taxpayers next to nothing), and can prove it with a form of state-sponsored certification showing they have emerged from the criminal justice system with formal training that serves everyone, lawbreaker or not;

- White-collars who have truly "given back" to and restored the community, even if such work while in the criminal justice system did not create restitution money for direct victim restitution.

- All stakeholders are civically engaged in all ways in this scenario (volunteering, giving, serving, associating);

- No minds are wasted.

*   *

b. **Business-World White-Collars Teaching Entrepreneurship to Lower Level Entrepreneurial Lawbreakers.**

There are many prison entrepreneurship training programs that do more than teach drug dealers how to be more effective upon release.[148] There are similarly many entrepreneurship training programs for the *formerly* incarcerated.

We felons have figured out that teaching skilled other-collars to make money in legitimate businesses is good business and therefore good public policy. And it solves the problem of depending on skeptical employers who don't want to hire people with criminal records for a variety of marginal to bad reasons.

A terrific example of the makings of a potentially even more terrific program is what seems the most successful and sophisticated program of its kind in the country: The Prison Entrepreneurship Program, in Texas.

---

[148] *See, e.g.*, Prison Entrepreneurship Guide, Inc. Magazine, (North Carolina, Ohio, Oklahoma, Oregon Texas). http://www.inc.com/articles/2009/02/prison-entrepreneurship_pagen_3.html

The organization is run partly by former
lawbreakers who have become entrepreneurs and
teachers. Their website describes what they do so
well and speaks for itself:

> We scour the Texas prison system, recruiting
> from more than 60 prisons, to handpick men
> with transformed hearts, impeccable work
> ethic and entrepreneurial potential.
>
> Applicants endure an intense application
> process; ..the Texas Department of Criminal
> Justice (TDCJ) transfers the eligible, pre-
> release men to the Cleveland Correctional
> Facility in Cleveland, Texas, where PEP
> operates.
>
> Most PEP participants were either dope
> dealers or violent criminals and many were
> raised in disadvantaged situations where
> education and achievement were not
> modeled.
>
> The participants receive a top-tier business
> education—they construct detailed pro-forma
> income statements, learn the relevance of
> EBITDA margins, take 40+ business exams
> and pitch their business concept 200+ times.
> They rub shoulders with more than 100
> executives in five months.
>
> For their final exam, participants deliver 30-
> minute oral business plan presentations to a
> judging panel of CEOs and venture capitalists
> from across the nation. Our graduation
> ceremony tops off the Business Plan
> Competition event as we celebrate, for the
> majority of the class, their first
> commencement ceremony ever.

We felons know the promise in such endeavors. The people who run the criminal justice system on a daily basis, and the legislators and other policy-makers who determine and control the resources that allow the criminal justice system to run, need better to understand the promise of enabling lawbreakers in such ways.

The missing piece, however, to the entrepreneurship training for lawbreakers industry, is that white-collars with entrepreneurship skills should be *required* as part of their criminal sentences to work for organizations like the Prison Entrepreneurship Program as teachers, while they are 'on paper,' in exchange for which these white-collar teachers should receive good time credit, or the like, from their sentences.

There is no reason to waste a mind by waiting for a skilled white-collar to complete a criminal sentence to civically engage him or her in entrepreneurship training for other-collars. That involvement should begin immediately upon and as part of the white-collar's sentence.

*   *

c. Fallen Lawyers: Lobbyists and Corn Farmers

Just like prison entrepreneurship programs teach former lawbreaker entrepreneurs to excel in business and to be self-sufficient, the public policy world is a sleeping giant of opportunity for non-business oriented lawbreakers and specifically for fallen lawyers.

There is no AA for ethically challenged lawyers. We are treated essentially like the lepers of the profession and often our communities, despite that we, too, are capable of reformation of character.[149]

---

[149] Redemption and reformation of character are recognized as core concepts in the Judeo-Christian tradition, but in practice seem generally recognized as valid only outside of criminal justice and employment. *See* Alfred Blumstein & Kiminori Nakamura, Redemption in the presence of widespread criminal background checks, 47 CRIMINOLOGY 327 (2009); *See also*, Patricia M. Harris & Kimberly S. Keller, Ex-Offenders Need Not Apply: The Criminal Background Check in Hiring Decisions, 21 J. CONTEMP. CRIM. JUST. 6 (2005).

We don't get lobotomies when we fall. Like other mortal fallen (or felons), often all we fallen lawyers need is a dose of socially acceptable redemption to make huge personal strides in the course of helping others.

Our redemption can be in many things, among them in civic engagement, which is accessible and always needed. One beauty of civic engagement is that people and the greater community always benefit.

My own redemption has been in civic engagement as a criminal justice reform lobbyist, advocate, professor and volunteer. I know civic engagement can be a redemptive force for other fallen lawyers like me. So I see great promise in the training of fallen lawyers as lobbyists. That's how we fallen lawyers can be corn farmers for the common good.

State bar regulators who operate the enforcement arms of the fifty state supreme courts have the opportunity greatly to advance the common good while creating prime opportunities for fallen lawyers to redeem themselves. Rather than simply punish offending lawyers, state bar regulators could offer distinctly redemptive opportunities for fallen lawyers to prove they are rehabilitated by encouraging lobbying for social justice agendas.

Lawyers in "law purgatory" (disciplinary exile without prison), incarcerated lawyers, and those on parole or probation retain vast education and skills when we leave practice the way everyone remembers how to ride a bike. That's a lot of collective mind not to waste.

Lobbying is not only one of the purest forms of civic engagement that fits fallen lawyers, it is also one of the few higher level activities in American culture which does not bar or regulate felons, because it is a legitimate activity protected by the First Amendment to the U.S. Constitution:

> "Congress shall make no law ... abridging the freedom of speech .... or the right of the people peaceably to assemble, and to petition the government for a redress of grievances."

Lobbying for me is about one thing: talking about what I know and about my passion: making things better for people with criminal records.

Lobbying for fallen lawyers presents fertile, legal ground to become practitioners on return to daily life; not practitioners of law but instead, practitioners of civic engagement.

Lobbying is not the practice of law[150] and it's far more than persuading legislators. Preparatory elements of lobbying include legal, public policy and legislative research and analysis, of both legislative and regulatory agendas.

Fallen lawyers can teach and do all of this, together with the larger part of lobbying that goes beyond directly persuading legislators: collaborating with and educating varied and disparate stakeholders or factions who are vested in the outcome and implementation of pending issues or imminent change.

Lobbying is so inherently "civic engagement," "democratic" and thus restorative that policymakers who run the state bar regulatory offices nationwide should consider the merits of social justice lobbying for fallen lawyers and educated lawbreakers as the potential "AA of lawyer reentry." It's legal, unregulated, and the demand is unlimited. Government doesn't slow down in terrible economies.

---

[150] Numerous statutes that define various forms or unauthorized practice of law expressly exclude lobbying.

Judges and administrators who run state supreme courts and prisons and who are serious about rehabilitation as a key component of their missions, should recognize that they have much to gain if not also a vested interest in training their fallen, or their inmates and releasees, parolees or probationers as social justice or non-profit sector lobbyists.

Few fallen lawyers or reasonably educated felons need more education than they have already when it comes to articulating in a persuasive manner the challenges, obstacles, and injustices people with criminal records face daily, and often for life.

When a person can speak authoritatively and with passion, people listen. That's why so many fallen lawyers and reasonably educated, or even moderately articulate felons can be good lobbyists. We don't need a script. And we needn't be too concerned about the Runyonesque mystique lobbyists have acquired from the media, urban myths, and true stories.

Nearly every American non-profit of substance and every small interest or association (as well as large and powerful ones) employs or retains lobbyists on a regular basis. Many non-profits profess to have social justice missions. Such organizations if true to their missions should seriously consider providing homes to lobbyists with criminal records who are committed to restoration and advancement of the common good through civic engagement and the advancement of diverse social justice agendas.

Specifically, closer to home, the needs of people with criminal records are no less legitimate than those of other non-business interests with enormous constituencies, like private and public foundation and charities, institutions of higher education, houses of worship, public interest groups of all kinds, mothers against drunk drivers, AARP, and all sorts of political bodies or entities, ranging from foreign governments, states, counties, and municipalities (all of whom employ lobbyists).

If empowered to do so as public policy advocates, appropriate (rehabilitated) people with criminal records like fallen lawyers, especially, can improve our communities and thereby restore a lot of the harm we caused, and a lot of harm we did not cause, too. But we must be in partnership with our legal system and criminal justice system. Otherwise, we are exiled and can heal or restore little.

Rehabilitated, fallen and recovering lawyers are among the perfect candidates to be agents in the lobbying process for the vast demographic of people with criminal records. So, too, are educated felons on their return from incarceration, parole or probation.

State bar regulators needn't hide in the ivory towers of running their judiciary branches, but instead should empower their fallen to flourish in the legislative branches for the restorative purpose of advancing the common good.

Fallen lawyers can help heal, too. Our supreme courts should enact rules that give us opportunities to return to do good, and incentive to prove our rehabilitation specifically by spending several years as social justice lobbyists. Such would be a true civically engaged partnership of different branches of government working together for the common good.

Lobbying is the advocacy of perspective by people or groups, so if that's a "special interest," so be it. People with criminal records couldn't possibly have a more acute perspective or more of a special interest. We represent nearly a third of America.

We have too many minds to waste.

CONCLUSION

Part of my purpose here has been to demonstrate that fixing our criminal justice system is one of our truly bi-partisan possibilities. I also told the story of how I fell so far and hard as a reminder we are all better than our worst acts. There are better solutions to right wrongs than some we employ today.

We felons have minds that should not be wasted, just like people without criminal records. Reformation of character and contribution to the common good is possible for many felons, too. Like my Senator friend said: "Most everyone has a background. Not everyone's background is memorialized."

The lack of a criminal record says nothing about a person's character, integrity, or work ethic. Sometimes a criminal record says far too much about a person who has one.

We are far more the same than different. I chose a mirror image for the title of this book, because in so many ways and as the poem on the following pages concludes:

"I am you—whenever you may or may not want me, too."

- MS -

I AM FIRST AMENDMENT

By Justice Greg Hobbs, Colorado Supreme Court. Reprinted by permission.

I am freedom of religion, freedom of speech, freedom of press, freedom to assemble, freedom to petition the government for redress of grievances.

I am Moses, Jesus, Gandhi, Martin Luther.

I am Joan of Arc, the Salem witches, the Hollywood writers summoned to appear before Senator McCarthy.

I am the man in Tiananmen Square staring down the gun barrel of a tank.

I am the Cathars burned at the stake, their mountain hideaways torn stone by stone by the French duke on orders from the Pope.

I am the Pope traveling to Communist Poland to be with his countrymen and women.

I am every man and woman who has said aloud, "This just isn't right!"

I am Jefferson yearning to have others see what is beyond the next mountain.

I am Lincoln full of strength for freeing others.

I am Roosevelt on the radio parting the drowning waters of fear.

I am Martin Luther King, Jr. praising the Lord and crying out for freedom in Selma, Alabama.

You can't plug me in or dial me up or shut me down.

You can't play me, display me, wrap me up in bubble wrap.

Every device that's ever been invented, every item that's ever been sold, every play or song or painting that's ever been born is my face and tongue and hand making, talking, inspiring, loving.

I am costly.

I am a young man gone down on land or sea or in the air to give the gift of living days so that others may.

I am Emily Dickinson shut up in her room because it wasn't seemly for women to be articulate publicly.

I am cheap, locked up, despised.

I am the bum in your street, the immigrant, the one they don't want in the Boy Scout Troop.

I am on your front porch wrapped in a rubber band, on the screen in the corner of your playroom, on your living room shelf.

I am what your children say to you and you to them.

I am what you don't like that others say and write.

I am you——whenever you may or may not want me, too.

*   *

ACKNOWLEDGEMENTS

For better or worse, my family of origin and the two mothers of my children, have all done their best when dealing with me at my worst. My children, Zoe Keziah, Marlee Jae and Judah Amichai, are my salvation. They ask me their questions about my background and circumstances (and other questions) when they seem ready to hear answers. So, I answer them. They think I'm kidding when I thank them for picking me as their father.

For the last 17 years, countless loved ones have blessed my family with unconditional love and support. There are too many marvelous people to acknowledge everyone by name, although I must mention a few with wedding planner trepidation.

Key people have offered invaluable friendship, loyalty, encouragement or feedback for countless versions of this text, notably: Judah Amichai, Jennifer Arndt, Wynne Bailey and her Dad (even when the Badgers were playing Nebraska), Howard Bernstein, Jody Chambers, Jack Coladarci, Claire Darch, Paul Fauteck, Clay Fong, Heywood Hoffman, Marlee Jae, Karen Lollar, Zoe Keziah, Peter Lubin, Philip Mostow, Ted Noyes, Rhonda Ntepp, Justin Paperny, Steve Paul, Vaughn Paul, Elizabeth Peters, Ethan Price, Stephen Richards, Vycki Rice, Richard Rowley,

Melanie Spitz, George Schueppert, Bryan Springmeyer, Carol Sweig, Julia Sweig, Luke Sydow, Mark Whitacre, Don Whitfield, Greg Williams, Rabbi Michael Zedek and Phil Zisook.

With "amazing grace," willing academics without whom I'd have remained truly lost and clueless how best to match my skills with my post-conviction future, have encouraged me as follows:

While I was still on probation, Glen Weissenberger, who was then Dean of the De Paul University College of Law, in Chicago, told me I had a worthy message and invited me to speak to legal ethics students.

Dean Weissenberger introduced me to Professor Michele Goodwin, who then taught Legal Ethics at De Paul and is now the Everett Fraser Professor in Law at the University of Minnesota. As to my daunting notion and Mike Coffield's prophecy that I would one day become a professor, Michele told me "don't count yourself out, buddy."

Professor Stephen Richards, now at the University of Wisconsin, Oshkosh, assured me in brief but meaningful correspondence I could indeed and should teach.

Professor Corinne Benedetto, Assistant Dean at the De Paul University School for New Learning hired me in 2000, and showed me I had an effective classroom voice and purpose.

My British history professor from freshman year in college at the University of Colorado, Chuck Middleton, emailed me one day to say he would soon become President of Roosevelt University, also in Chicago, where ultimately over 19 consecutive terms between 2003 and 2010, I taught 31 courses as a legal studies professor.

Professors LiYing Li and Karen Lollar, both at Metropolitan State College of Denver, welcomed me respectively into the Criminal Justice and Criminology, and Communications Arts Departments when I returned to Colorado from Chicago.

In the public policy world, my debts beyond words extend to the following people who have honored me with their respect, patience, teaching and insights when we have worked together rubbed shoulders, and sometimes vehemently disagreed:

Diane Williams and Veronica Cunningham of the Safer Foundation, who bet on me, hired me as Public Policy Liaison, and sent me to the Illinois Capitol. Rev. Al Sharp and Walter Boyd of Protestants for the Common Good, both teachers, friends and lobbying collaborators. Chicago attorney Tom Grippando, a thoughtful and wise policy mentor.

Illinois lobbyists Terry Steczo and Maureen Mulhall are in a class by themselves. So are Senate President John Cullerton and his Legal Counsel, Jim Dodge, Sen. William Haine, Sen. John Millner, Sen. Michael Noland, Sen. Kwame Raoul, Sen. AJ Wilhelmi, Sen. Dale Righter, Rep. Barbara Currie, Rep. Sara Feigenholtz, Rep. Constance "Connie" Howard, Rep. LaShawn Ford, Rep. Dennis Reboletti, Rep. Chapin Rose, and Mark Warnsing, GOP Legal Counsel to the Illinois Senate Criminal Law Committee.

At my 35th Boulder High School reunion, Denver writer Eliza Cross inspired my final push with key information, insights and encouragement.

*   *

ABOUT THE AUTHOR

Michael Sweig is founder of the Institute for People with Criminal Records, a Colorado-based not-for-profit that provides advocacy and academic support for criminal justice reform agendas nationwide.

He recently returned to Colorado after 28 years in Chicago as a lawyer, legal studies professor, and lobbyist.

Michael teaches in both the Criminal Justice and Communications Arts departments at Metropolitan State College of Denver. He volunteers in the City of Boulder Restorative Justice program, and is creator and producer of various media works entitled "Beyond Felony.™"

In August 2010, The Chicago Tribune covered Michael in "From Practicing Law to Changing it," by Dawn Turner Trice, Chicago Tribune August 1, 2010.

Michael was co-author and the principal lobbyist for Illinois Senate Bill 1050, 96th General Assembly (2009), which Governor Pat Quinn called "noble" legislation. Effective January 1, 2010, Senate Bill 1050 (P.A. 96-852) put Illinois in a class by itself for the sweeping remedies it provides people with criminal records to prove their rehabilitation, and the protections it gives employers to hire them. He is working on a similar bill in the Colorado legislature.

In September 2010, the Illinois Senate President appointed Michael to the Illinois Criminal Justice Information Authority Task Force on Inventorying Employment Restrictions.

In September 2009, Illinois State Rep. Constance A. "Connie" Howard recognized "Doc" Sweig "for his invaluable contribution to legislative initiatives designed to assist those who have paid their debt to society and seek a second chance to become productive citizens..."

Michael Sweig has been disbarred on consent from the Illinois Bar since summer 1998. He voluntarily turned himself in for previously resolved client trust account violations, pleaded guilty to a felony, and completed a 48-month probation sentence that included one year of home confinement and 500 hours of community service. Michael has been eligible in Illinois to petition for reinstatement of his law license since Summer 2001.

On request, Mr. Sweig will provide a copy of an affidavit submitted by his former law partner, in 2007, in opposition to Mr. Sweig's pursuit of a certificate of rehabilitation under the law which Mr. Sweig later rewrote and lobbied for passage as noted above. The affidavit contains more extensive and underlying details of Mr. Sweig's crimes. Mr. Sweig withdrew his request for a certificate of rehabilitation – without prejudice – not long after Judge Paul Biebel informed him in Court that Mr. Sweig's lawyer, Mike Coffield, had died the night before.

Visit PeoplewithCriminalRecords.org

Michael Sweig

NOTES:

Made in the USA
Charleston, SC
14 June 2012